SWORD FIGHTING
A MANUAL FOR ACTORS & DIRECTORS

Other Applause Favorites

THE APPLAUSE
FIRST FOLIO OF SHAKESPEARE

THE INDIVIDUAL FOLIO TEXTS

THE APPLAUSE
SHAKESPEARE LIBRARY

WILLIAM SHAKESPEARE:
A POPULAR LIFE

ACTING SHAKESPEARE
BY JOHN GIELGUD

SHAKESPEARE'S PLAYS
IN PERFORMANCE

SHAKESCENES:
SHAKESPEARE FOR TWO

SOLILOQUY: THE
SHAKESPEARE MONOLOGUES

SWORD FIGHTING
A MANUAL FOR ACTORS & DIRECTORS

KEITH DUCKLIN & JOHN WALLER

Illustrated by
Keith Ducklin & Adam des Forges

Sword Fighting:
A Manual for Actors and Directors
Copyright © *Keith Ducklin & John Waller 2001*
Illustrations © Keith Ducklin & Adam des Forges
Previously published in Great Britain by Robert Hale Ltd.

Library of Congress Cataloging-in-Publication Data

Library of Congress Catalog Number: 2001087839

ISBN 1-55783-459-8

APPLAUSE THEATRE BOOKS
151 W46th Street, 8th Floor
New York, NY 10036
Phone: (212) 575-9265
FAX: (646) 562-5852
email: info@applausepub.com
internet: www.applausepub.com

SALES & DISTRIBUTION, HAL LEONARD CORP.
7777 West Bluemound Road, P.O. Box 13819
Milwaukee, WI 53213
Phone: (414) 774-3630 Fax: (414) 774-3259
email: halinfo@halleonard.com
internet: www.halleonard.com

Cover photos provided by Arms of Valor, Ltd. visit them online at:
www.armsofvalor.com or call toll free 1-888-477-9673

Cover photo (bottom left) from Shakespeare & Company's 2000 season Mainstage production of Romeo and Juliet directed by Cecil MacKinnon. Pictured: Jason Asprey as Mercutio. Photo by Kevin Sprague of Studio Two Design. Photograph courtesy of Shakespeare & Company.

Contents

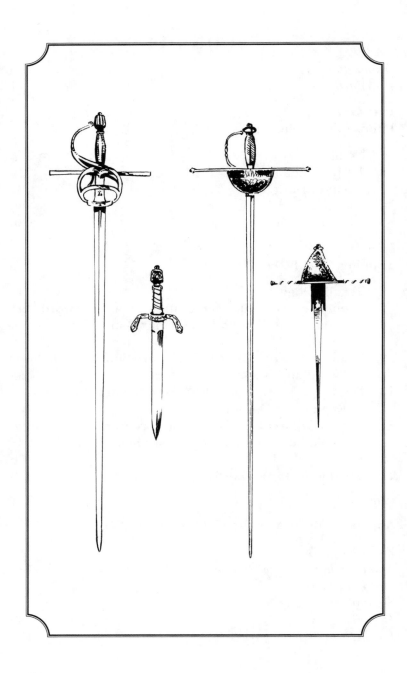

Disclaimer

This book contains advice on the practical use of historical weapons and the recreation of their associated fighting styles for both martial arts training and stage-combat purposes. Any persons wishing to practise the techniques shown in this book do so at their own risk. Any persons wishing to train with historical weapons or recreate their associated fighting styles, including the techniques shown in this book, are advised to seek medical confirmation first as to whether or not they should attempt such activities.

SWORD FIGHTING

Keith Ducklin has spent fifteen years as a practitioner of period fighting techniques, having studied with John Waller. He taught dramatic combat at some of England's top drama schools and directed many fights for the London fringe theatre circuit until 1994, when he became involved with the Royal Armouries Museum. He has fought in full fifteenth-century plate armour before both Her Majesty Queen Elizabeth II and HRH The Prince of Wales; demonstrated medieval European swordfighting in Japan and has made many television appearances demonstrating historical fighting styles. He is an accredited teaching member of the British Academy of Dramatic Combat, secretary of the European Historical Combat Guild, and continues to train students of swordsmanship in Britain and America.

John Waller has spent more than thirty years as an action arranger and historical consultant for stage and screen. For nineteen years he taught stage combat at drama schools including the London Academy of Music and Drama and the Guildhall School of Music and Drama. His work on the uses of armour and weapons brought him to the *Mary Rose* and its archery finds. As Head of Interpretation for the Royal Armouries at Leeds he has helped to produce many specialist film projects. He is a member of the British Academy of Dramatic Combat and the Equity Fight Director's Register, and in 1999 founded the European Historical Combat Guild. His numerous stage, film and TV credits include, amongst many others, *Martin Guerre, Elizabeth R, Dr Who* and *Pride and Prejudice* and *Arms In Action.*

Acknowledgements

From Keith Ducklin

To John Waller, who set me on this road, and to my great friend and colleague Andrew Deane, my first and best opponent; to Guy Wilson, Master of the Royal Armouries; also fight directors Mike Loades and Rodney Cottier; Mike Finn Sensei and Sifu Nigel Sutton; to Adam des Forges, for helping me with the illustrations; and to John Hale, who gave me this chance to see my first book in print.

From John Waller:

To Ewart Oakeshott, whose love of the lore of arms has inspired so many scholars of arms and armour; to those drama schools and colleges who continue to support the training of their students according to the principles laid out in this book, and to my son Jonathan, who has always fought, shot and stood at my side.

Actors who, in every other case, are most particular about historical accuracy, generally dispose of all questions relative to fighting by referring them to the first fencing-master at hand; and accordingly one sees Laertes and Hamlet with the utmost *sang-froid* going through a 'salute' which, besides being perfectly unmanageable with rapiers, was only established in all details some fifty years ago. There would be less anachronism in uncorking a bottle of champagne to fill the king's beaker than there is in Hamlet correctly lunging, reversing his point, saluting carte and tierce etc – foil fencing, in fact – in spite of the anticipation raised by Osric's announcement that the bout should be played with rapier and dagger.

From the Introduction to *Schools and Masters of Fence*
by Egerton Castle, 1885

Introduction

Sword Fighting: A Manual for Actors and Directors has been written to offer some guidelines on how to train with historical weapons, as well as showing how authentic European fighting styles from the past can be adapted for the purpose of directing combats for stage, screen and living history projects in the twenty-first century.

It is the authors' belief that too little modern fight choreography accurately reflects the way our ancestors fought, even though there has never been a greater body of research available from which the fight director can draw in devising exciting and authentic historical combats. While no conscientious director would accept gas-light in a period setting which calls for candles, or a waltz instead of a pavane, there are far fewer who know the difference between a sword fight based on modern fencing techniques and one derived accurately from historical fighting styles. Making this difference clear should be one of the most important aspects of any fight director's job, and directors who demand their performers' costume and deportment be as accurate as possible should ensure that their cast members are being advised on the correct period weapons by someone who knows how to use them. Likewise, performers who undertake to bring to life experienced fighters in a dramatic production – and who will only have a limited amount of time for weapons training no matter how keen they may be to explore this important facet of their characters' background – should demand a fight director capable of training them to the highest possible standard in the time available.

It follows that to meet these challenges, the job of the fight director must be twofold: firstly, to help make clear how any given script indicates the characters' motivation and physical condition; and secondly, to bring the fight alive using well-researched and historically accurate techniques. Accordingly, Part One of this book lays down a positive philosophy for training; Part Two provides illustrated step-by-step training sequences to aid the reader in recreating the fighting styles of some of the most commonly used swords from the late Middle Ages to the end of the eighteenth century. Each sequence is based on techniques suggested by a range of original fighting manuals from that particular period.

To sum up, then, this is a book to be read by those seeking authenticity as well as excitement in their fight choreography. Certainly, no manual of this type can hope to survey every aspect of Europe's martial heritage, but it is hoped that this book will prove useful in giving the reader a better understanding of the diverse dramatic opportunities afforded by a realistic approach to bringing historical fighting techniques to life.

On a final, literary, note, there are many female sword enthusiasts, as well as fight directors, and it is only for reasons of clarity that the male pronoun has been exclusively used throughout this book.

Keith Ducklin and John Waller
Leeds, 2000

PART ONE

Philosophy – John Waller

1 'Reality First'

The techniques described in this book are the product of a system developed over a thirty-year period of teaching historical weaponry, as well as directing fights for stage and screen. It emphasizes 'reality first'; in other words, that all techniques taught should have their basis in those realistic options available to the combatants with the weapons at their disposal.

When I first began experimenting with historical weapons and techniques, long before I took up fight arranging and teaching as a career, there was nothing approaching the interest in European martial arts that is evident today. Access to research material was much harder to obtain, even if you had some idea of where to look. Today there is a wealth of information available not only in book form but also on the Internet, whereas at that time there were no computers or even photocopiers to help you record the information when you found something interesting.

Growing up in the 1950s, one source of inspiration for me were the popular historical and swashbuckling films of the day, although, as I got older, I realized that most fight directors during that period, including the legendary Hollywood names, were fencing masters who were adapting their sporting techniques as far as possible to give a flavour of the past. I always felt there was something missing in this approach because although these fencing masters choreographed superb routines (especially for films set in the eighteenth and nineteenth centuries), they were often guilty of sacrificing reality by having fighters from stories set in earlier periods using lightweight blades – even though they might be mounted in the correct period hilts.

I believed strongly that instead of adapting period weapons for use with modern fencing movements, the better method would be to make accurate copies of the original weapons and see what sort of movement styles would naturally develop. With this idea in mind, I began to define my system and in the early 1960s came together with a group of several like-minded archers, swordsmen, horsemen and falconers to form the Medieval Society, which still exists today. As the years passed I was able to search out and study some of the original fighting manuals and only then did I realize that everything I had come to believe was borne out by the descriptions and illustrations of the original masters.

However, it was less my study of swordsmanship than my reputation as an archery champion, falconer and horseman that eventually brought me into the entertainment world as historical adviser for films and television shows with historical backgrounds. Given these opportunities of putting my theories into practice, I determined that I would make a speciality of arranging action sequences in which reality came first and theatricality second. In *Monty Python and the Holy Grail*, for instance, the Python team, having been shown the authentic use of weapons in the medieval period, insisted that the fight itself was kept as realistic as possible, in contrast to the film's many comic elements. Later, for the fights for the fantasy *Hawk the Slayer*, the director had the action of the Japanese samurai films in mind, even though the overall production design was distinctly European. My solution was to base the sword techniques of Hawk (John Terry), Voltan (Jack Palance) and the rest of the cast on those taught by the medieval German master-at-arms Hans Talhoffer. Talhoffer, like many other European masters throughout history, taught techniques which had elements in common with those of other warrior cultures across the world, including the Japanese.

My stage work has also provided many interesting challenges. For an unconventional production of *Macbeth* staged by Declan Donellan's Cheek by Jowl theatre company, I was asked to train the fighters with authentically weighted and balanced medieval weapons, only for the actors to dispense with them at the end of the rehearsal period – the reason was that every object apparently used in the production was to be mimed, including the swords! What Declan wanted, of course, was for the audience to experience the power and intention of a real sword fight, even though the actors had no weapons in their hands. When I worked with Sir Ian McKellen on his National Theatre production of *Richard III*, he wanted to wear a full harness of steel in rehearsals, so that he could try to experience to some extent the reality of the late fifteenth-century armoured combat. Most recently I was asked by the West Yorkshire Playhouse to direct the specially filmed 'Duelling Cavalier' movie scenes used in their stage production of *Singin' in the Rain*. This time I had to choreograph a fight, not with the authentic styles of the seventeenth century, but with the heightened reality of those very swashbuckling films which had thrilled me when I was young.

Equally as important as my film and theatre contacts were those I found amongst the archaeological and academic communities. I was fortunate in being asked by the Royal Armouries to assist in the production of two influential films on the uses of armour and weapons: *How a Man Schall be Armyd* (showing the dressing of a man in a complete original sixteenth-century armour) and *Masters of Defence* (a history of swordsmanship from the fifteenth to the nineteenth century). When in 1995 the Master of the Armouries, Guy Wilson, went ahead with the decision to move much of the collection from the Tower of London to its new location in the city of Leeds, his knowledge of my work led to my appointment as Head of Interpretation, helping the museum incorporate into its visitor experience a continuing programme of live combat demonstrations and specially commissioned films on arms and armour.

Finally, bringing things full circle, by the mid 1970s when stage combat replaced fencing on the curriculum of many drama schools, I had the opportunity to test my movement theories fully in a class situation. My system produced excellent results and became extremely popular amongst students. As time went on I was invited to teach at many drama schools and colleges, and teaching has continued to play an important part in my life over the years, bringing me inspiration and satisfaction.

Throughout my career, the guiding principles on which I originally based my system have remained unchanged. I believe that before either teaching the use of a particular weapon, or working on the staging of a fight, the fight director must ask how the weapon's use will be affected by:

- the mechanics of the human body;
- the design of the weapon;
- the clothing or protection worn by the fighters;
- the combatants' motivation.

Only then can he begin to examine the fight's dramatic requirements.

2 Body Mechanics

If a fight is to be exciting, believable, and yet safe, everyone involved should be aware of two things: firstly, that though the people in the script are capable of committing acts of violence, the actors or actresses themselves must always be in total control of their actions; and secondly, that while the aggression generated on stage or before the camera should appear real to the audience, those watching should only ever believe that the characters are in danger, never the performers. The most productive method for achieving this understanding lies in persuading the performers that if their characters are supposedly skilled fighters, their portrayals are unlikely to appear truthful unless they can use their weapons effectively.

It is clear from surviving contemporary fight manuals that sword masters down the centuries urged their students to perfect their techniques, and with good reason: by the medieval period the European warrior class had dominated both the social and political order of Western Europe for many centuries, and this ascendancy had been achieved through the use of highly developed and efficient methods of fighting, both armed and unarmed. Swordsmanship continued to be an accomplishment expected from the military and civilians of the upper classes until the early part of the nineteenth century, and skill with both sword and lance was still practised by the cavalry of many European countries until the twentieth century.

My system is based on certain basic principles of body mechanics, many of which are borne out by the old European manuals as well as being shared by other martial arts around the world. I assess each fighter on an individual basis, making sure that whether (s)he is tall or short, big or small, fast moving or slow, the techniques taught will suit their particular physicality.

Clearly, the distinction must be made between students of the past, who were being taught offensive and defensive techniques for use in what might be life-threatening situations, and those of the 2000s who are never likely to find themselves using a sword in real combat. Nevertheless, anyone involved in recreating period fighting styles ought to appreciate how very strongly the psychological state of those of our ancestors who lived by the sword must have been affected by the necessity of being prepared to die by it.

All weapons training should encourage combatants to become aware of their bodies' responses when carrying out the various physical actions of attack and defence, and how these responses can be controlled. This awareness can be experienced from the beginning of training if the students ensure that all offensive or defensive actions are made with eye contact, balance and intent.

Eye contact

This means the combatants' eyes are focused on their opponents' from the beginning to the end of the fight, simultaneously taking in the greatest possible range of visual information from other areas. They are, in fact, developing their peripheral vision. In reality, peripheral vision would have allowed the combatant to react instinctively to danger from more than one quarter, to anticipate their opponent's attacks rather than simply responding to them, and to be aware of when and where their opponent might be vulnerable. For stage combat purposes, developing an instinctive awareness of movement allows combatants to work together with confidence, monitoring not just each others' movements, but also whatever else is happening around them.

Balance

This is vital if the student is to keep control of body and weapon: whether attacking or defending, they should always maintain a sure footing.

The attacker should lead with the weapon and follow with the body, the foot landing at the same moment as the blow. This allows him to strike with the desired amount of force while ensuring that he does not over-commit to the attack.

The defender should lead with the body, the foot landing at the same moment as he makes a strong and balanced block, beat counter-attack or attack; alternatively he can avoid the blow altogether by moving out of range. Leading with the body ensures the defender gives himself as much time as possible to respond.

Intent

This describes the level of power behind each strike, and therefore its intended depth of penetration, as well as the corresponding level of energy behind each defence. Unlike eye-contact and balance, the level of intent must be adjusted for training and performance in the interests of safety.

In reality, the energy expended on each attack will not only carry the blow to its intended depth of penetration, but also power the follow-through, the continuation of the weapon's movement into the most advantageous position from which to renew the attack or prepare a defence against a counter-attack. The level of intent also determines whether the defender will try to block, beat or avoid. When blocking, the defender should meet the attacker's weapon with sufficient power to prevent it dashing his own aside, but without any excess of force which might leave him unable to effect either a counter-attack or a further defence. A beat deflects an opponent's attack and in doing so sends the defender's sword into a position for an immediate counter-attack. Avoidances, usually from the most powerful and fully committed attacks, depend on the correct estimation of timing, direction and distance. Intent is therefore one of the most important factors in a fight – both in reality and for training and stage-combat purposes.

During training, rehearsal and performance, however, certain safety adjustments must be introduced. The attacker must never assume that his opponent will make the correct defence, and so must change the point at which any cut or thrust reaches what in reality would be its target, to another point either short of, or away from, the defender's body. The defender, meanwhile, must never assume that the attacker will make the correct adjustment to his strike, and should therefore block, beat or avoid as though the attack had been aimed on target and with real intent. It should be noted that because blocked attacks have their flow of energy interrupted, follow-through will never occur in training or performance except when an attack is intended to fail because of an avoidance by the defender: when making these moves the attacker should still deliver the blow as though he had expected to strike his opponent.

It can sometimes happen that the repetition of training or performance leads to the combatants losing their intent in some of the moves in the fight. This can only be detrimental to both the performers' safety and the audience's sense of belief. The only remedy is for the combatants to remind themselves constantly of the *real* as well as the *adjusted* intent of each blow.

This method of encouraging those involved in the fight scene to become familiar with the mechanics of the human body will increase their instinctive understanding of the mental and physical logic of attack and defence. This in turn allows them to handle the weapons with awareness under pressure, making it clear how the various elements of any staged fight should be rooted in reality.

The next factor to be taken into consideration is the variation of physical type and condition amongst the cast, because people have always varied in their physical characteristics and the choreography of the fight should reflect the advantages and disadvantages encountered by the combatants as a result of their physical disparities. Sometimes the lack of attention to these factors when casting can make reality harder to achieve. The title role in *Macbeth* for instance, is one often thought to require the acting skills of a mature and experienced performer sometimes in middle-age and not always fit enough to portray physically the character Shakespeare suggests. If the fight director is faced with an inexperienced or out of condition Macbeth against a fit or well-trained Macduff, everyone involved may have to work much harder for the result Shakespeare clearly intended.

This said, performers with good physical backgrounds do not automatically make the best fighters. For example, there has circulated for many years a piece of received wisdom which suggests that training in modern fencing is good preparation for stage combat. This makes little sense, considering that the type of fencing practised today has virtually nothing left in common with the art of swordsmanship, having become an opportunistic sport in which the combatants are trained to hit one another with weapons of highly specialized design, wearing body protection to avoid the danger of injury! Better equipped are those performers who have taken stage combat lessons in the course of their drama training, or have been previously involved in fight scenes in the course of their careers – though it must be said that the beliefs and techniques taught by some fight directors differ markedly from those espoused here. Dancers are usually in very good physical shape and have a relaxed yet precise sense of movement which means they can sometimes take well to combat training; the fight director must ensure that he keeps the psychological aspects of the fight in mind and resists the temptation to make the routine an exercise in pure movement. Those who show enthusiasm and commitment usually prove the most adaptable and reliable fighters – even when they have had little or no previous stage combat or movement training.

3   Weapon Design

The design of the swords to be used in a production is important because their weight, hilt form and type of blade will dictate how they can be used to the best effect.

To take an historical example, throughout the early medieval period knightly fighting swords were generally broad-bladed and used more often for cutting than thrusting. They were heavy weapons, designed to deliver a powerful blow against an opponent who was very often wearing body protection made from some strong yet flexible material such as mail and/or thick padding. Even if the blow did not penetrate the armour it would transmit the shock through to the body beneath, causing damage to tissue and bone. Because of the weight of both swords and armour, fighters needed to keep their balance while putting the maximum power into their attacks and defences, and I believe medieval fighters who intended using their weapons in earnest would have trained just as systematically as, for instance, the small-sword fighters of the eighteenth century, because the results of losing a fight with either weapons could have been equally serious. If a fight is choreographed with correctly weighted replicas of medieval swords, the performers will, of course, need to get used to these weight and movement factors in a relatively short period of time; however, I believe that with the correct training they should have no trouble learning a safe, effective routine so long as the fight director has a proper understanding of how efficiently these swords were used in their own time.

When all this is considered, it seems unfortunate that we still see stage and screen fights – even in productions where the effort has actually been made to procure well-made replica swords and armour of earlier periods – perpetuating the erroneous impression that both the swords and their users were clumsy and ill-balanced.

The nomenclature of swords and other edged weapons is a study in itself and constantly debated by experts. Regardless of what names they are given and however stylishly they are embellished, fighting swords have always been designed and constructed for practical use. Since this book is primarily about sword techniques we will confine ourselves to the most basic names for the weapons we are going to study: *medieval two-handed sword; medieval hand-and-a-half-sword; sixteenth-century single-handed sword and buckler; sixteenth- and seventeenth-century rapier and dagger;* and *late seventeenth-century transition rapier/eighteenth-century smallsword.*

By the early medieval period even fighters who equipped themselves with helms, mail, textile padding and shields were not guaranteed complete protection against strong and well-delivered attacks from swords. If a blow could not be avoided, the shield was the fighter's next defence – this could cover half the body and the challenge was how the attacker could get around an opponent's shield to deliver a blow without leaving himself vulnerable. By the late Middle Ages, fighters who could afford the expense were wearing armour of plate (solid sections of metal) designed to deflect attacking weapons. This may be a reason why shields appear to have been carried less frequently at this time. Certainly the deflective quality of plate meant that cutting blows were rendered much less effective, but thrusts could still cause serious injury, especially if aimed at areas such as the face, armpits or groin. The hand-and-a-half was a type of sword longer than the single-hander and which could be used effectively both on foot and from horseback. It was so-called because when used on foot it was often held in both hands, one hand wholly on the grip, the other hand half on the grip and half on the pommel. Many hand-and-a-halfs seem to have been specifically designed for attacking armoured men, with rigid, tapering blades ideal for thrusting into the areas of an opponent's body unprotected by plate, though they were still used to cut. The sword could also be grasped by the blade for certain techniques: swung like an axe or hook using the cross-guard to attack; or turned pommel forward to deliver a punching blow (this is the origin of the expression to give someone a 'pummelling' which is sometimes still used today to describe the action of repeatedly hitting an opponent without pausing). To make stronger parries or give greater control when attacking at close quarters the sword could be held with one hand on the grip and the other on the blade. Fighters also learned grappling and throwing techniques.

The two-handed sword shared the characteristics of the hand-and-a-half, but had an even longer blade which gave the fighter an advantage at long range. However, this extra length meant it could only be used effectively by fighters on foot.

Throughout the medieval period and into the sixteenth century, soldiers and civilians often used broad-bladed cut-and-thrust swords in conjunction with hand-held shields called bucklers. The buckler was used to deflect an opponent's attack, or to deal a punching blow to the opponent himself. By the late sixteenth century, however, the combination of sword and buckler was regarded as being more suitable for use by soldiers and those of the lower classes, while the swept-hilted rapier was adopted as the sword of the gentleman.

The swept-hilt developed during the 1500s when a series of rings and bars were added to the sword hilt to give the hand greater protection. This was the period when fire-arms were making full plate-armour redundant on the battle-field, and the new, more protective hilt may have been intended to take the place of the metal gauntlet.

Some swept-hilts retained broad cut-and-thrust blades, while other types were developed with lighter, narrower blades as thrusting came to be regarded by many masters as a faster and more efficient method of attacking than cutting (though disabling cuts could still be inflicted with these blades). The rapier was often used in conjunction with a dagger, which in addition to blocking or trapping an opponent's blade, could be used to slash and stab. It was taken for granted that a fighter would use every opportunity to pommel, punch, kick, trip or wrestle his opponent. The cloak, fashionable item of civilian dress, was sometimes used in defence: partially wrapped around the arm it gave some protection and could be used to entrap an opponent's weapons and prevent him from making an effective defence, or could be thrown at him.

By the mid-seventeenth century another style of rapier made its appearance: the cup-hilt. Instead of the bars of the swept-hilt, this sword had a solid, cupped guard, a cross, and a single swept bar, or knuckle-bow, to protect the fingers and back of the hand. Cup-hilts are the type of swords so beloved of twentieth-century fight directors that they have shown up in films set a hundred years before and after the period in which they were actually carried. In fact they had one of the shortest lives of any sword pattern, because by the close of the century the hilts and blades of civilian swords had been steadily reduced in weight and dimensions to form what are generally referred to as transition rapiers.

Throughout the eighteenth century the rapier continued to be reduced in size and weight until it evolved into the smallsword. This weapon and another called the spadroon (a cut-and-thrust weapon often favoured by travellers and sometimes carried by soldiers) were the last swords to be carried openly in western Europe as items of civilian dress. The smallsword generally had a light and narrow triangular blade, not sharp along its edge but tapering to a sharp point. It had a shallow guard no bigger than the palm of a hand, finger rings (which on later smallswords were often purely decorative), a small cross and a knuckle-bow. The smallsword was designed almost exclusively for thrusting, though slashing cuts could be made with the tip. Some masters still taught grappling techniques.

Obtaining modern reproductions of these weapons should not present any problem – at least in Europe – as specialist theatrical or living history suppliers can now be located in many countries. It should be noted however that the quality, durability and authenticity of the weapons on offer can vary greatly. Theatrical weapons are usually supplied with steel or aluminium blades which give an authentic sound during a live performance, while for film and TV, fibreglass is sometimes substituted – the sounds of blade contact being added post-production by the sound technicians. Regardless of the material supplied, the fight director should still ensure that the techniques choreo-graphed are based on those possible with swords made from steel and of the correct weight.

The fight director should be asked to advise on the initial choice of swords to ensure that they are well-proportioned, correctly balanced and in good overall condition. Spare swords should always be ordered, and a careful watch kept on how well each sword stands up to repeated use. Faulty swords are a danger to the performers and the audience and should *never* be used: instead, they should be sent back to the suppliers for replacement. However, blades of any material are liable to chipping and regular attention should be given to removing burrs from the edges. Otherwise, regular cleaning and maintenance of blades and hilts should ensure that they give good service.

4   Clothing and Protection

Clothing and body protection has always affected, and in turn been affected by, the weapons carried by fighters and the way in which those weapons were used.

From the time swords first appeared, various forms of body protection began to be worn to limit the injury these weapons could inflict. New variations of sword design, and also new techniques for their use were then developed to penetrate the body protection, and so on; however, it should be remembered that body protection was intended to give the fighter a combination of protection and manoeuvrability. No sensible fighter would have put on protective clothing of any kind unless he believed it would actually improve his chances for survival.

Fashionable dress was also significant, because the individual characteristics of civilian combat styles from different periods often developed as a result of the clothing worn by the combatants in their everyday lives. For example, during the sixteenth century, it became fashionable to wear a sword as part of everyday dress. This changed the wearer's body space, and meant that on many occasions, his movement had to accommodate manoeuvring a long weapon in its scabbard in and out of doorways, up and down stairs, and through gatherings of people. When bowing, he had to be careful he did not grip the sword hilt in such a way that the scabbard was raised up behind him and struck someone! The clichéd theatrical bow, right hand in the air, left hand down by the side, dates back to the time when the right hand was used for salutation and the left controlled the sword's position. Although swords and scabbards could be removed for comfort when seated, this was not always done, and fighters who had reason to be suspicious of their surroundings developed ways of sitting and rising quickly while still wearing their weapons. The performers' knowledge of these factors should affect their characters' movement throughout the play, not just in the fight scenes.

Many materials have been used throughout history in the construction of body protection, including textiles, leather, metal, or a combination of all three. The most protective material of all was steel, and some cavalry regiments were still riding into battle wearing cuirasses (breastplates) during the early stages of the First World War.

The adverse effects of wearing armour on a fighter's stamina and manoeuvrability are very often over-emphasized. For instance, the image of the European man-at-arms throughout the Middle Ages as a lumbering mass of metal, barely able to defend himself and unable to rise if knocked to the ground, is a popular misconception. A late medieval harness (suit of armour) was composed of both plate (solid metal sections) and mail (interlinking iron rings) and generally weighed between 70 and 80lb (35–40kg). A modern British infantry soldier sometimes carries to the battlefield weapons, body armour and other equipment weighing over 100lb (50kg) – although he sheds much of this weight before he fights. A fit man of the medieval period, trained to be a warrior since boyhood, would not have found a harness excessively heavy to bear and the weight was spread over the body by having each of the plates attached to an arming-doublet (a thickly padded undergarment) as closely as possible to the areas they were designed to defend. Despite some restrictions, the wearer was able to move relatively easily on foot or on horseback.

Not every actor or actress will have the chance (or the physicality or inclination) to spend many hours of rehearsal or performance in an authentically reproduced harness: consequently, modern stage and screen armour is rarely made from the correct materials. Painted knitted string is often used for mail, while plate is frequently made either from fibreglass or aluminium. The advantages of these materials are obvious: they are lighter and generally more comfortable than steel when worn over long periods. However, their appearance can be a drawback, especially now that re-enactment societies, heritage sites and museums in many countries regularly offer their public the opportunity to see and touch replica armour of steel from all periods. String mail in particular rarely looks convincing, but unfortunately there is no better lightweight substitute available at the time of writing; plate armour of fibreglass appears very drab unless patinated by being given an application of stove-polish and then buffed; while aluminium, though it can be made to look both handsome and realistic, is a soft metal which may need a great deal of attention for dents and bends after a fight scene. This said, for those performers and directors determined to work with as near as possible the real article, there are now a number of armourers across Europe and the United States capable of making good quality reproduction mail and plate in steel.

If the decision has been made not to have authentic armours specially created for the production, the fighters will have to be equipped from costumiers' stock. It takes a knowledgeable and conscientious wardrobe person to outfit any number of performers properly from what may be available, and wherever possible the fight director ought to be on hand to see that no one is sent away with anything that is ill-fitting or out of period. At this stage it is worth everyone involved bearing in mind that historically even low-quality armour would have been altered and/or padded to fit the wearer so that it gave not only the maximum amount of protection, but also as much comfort and freedom of movement as possible: taking the same trouble when fitting out the performers may well result in a better fight scene.

Armour was not usually worn in everyday life by civilians of any period (though travellers and duellists sometimes wore concealed mail shirts as late as the close of the eighteenth century). Instead, civilians who found themselves beset by attackers relied on their fighting skills alone for defence. Some items of period clothing created unique problems. Throughout the sixteenth century, for example, leg coverings changed from the close-fitting medieval fashion to a much more voluminous cut. Fighting manuals of the period show swordsmen keeping their weapons held away from the body, and fighters wearing accurate reproductions of such costume may soon experience the problems that can arise if the swords and daggers are held too close and become entangled in the extra fabric. By the mid-eighteenth century, leg coverings were again tighter fitting, but as wearing modern reproductions has shown, the correct period cut is essential if fighters are to have the stretch on their lunges suggested by the contemporary manuals.

Other items proved more advantageous. During the late sixteenth and much of the seventeenth century, cloaks of varying lengths were regular worn as part of civilian dress, usually tied over the left shoulder and under the right to leave the sword-arm free. Fighters sometimes used their cloaks instead of their daggers for defence, wrapping a length of the material around the non sword-arm and using the remainder to trap or deflect their opponents' weapons. The cloak could also be thrown at an opponent. In the nineteenth century, swords ceased to be worn as part of civilian dress, but gentlemen rarely walked out without their canes. Fencing schools taught adaptations of sword techniques for use with the cane against attackers, and many canes were in fact sword-sticks with blades concealed inside them.

Good quality period clothing is far less difficult to obtain than armour, but priority should still be given to getting the fighters costumes which fit well and offer no unnecessary hindrances to movement. Shoes and boots should be given extra special consideration, because well-maintained footwear is essential for the fighters' safety and comfort. The soles and heels should be in a good state of repair and newly soled with *high quality non-slip soles*. If any fighter's footwear is supplied in a degraded condition or without proper soling it should either be rejected or sent to a shoe repairer – preferably one with experience of preparing footwear for films and shows – before the beginning of costumed rehearsals. Those involved in the fight scene who ignore these precautions risk the safety of both performers and audience, and where safety is a factor there should *never* be any compromise.

Performers should also be made aware of the correct way to wear their weapons and move around with them. The fight director should be called on to advise on this. Most early medieval swords were strapped to the wearer with belts attached directly to the scabbards. They sat on the left hip, slightly angled forward so they could be controlled and drawn easily. Later swords were usually suspended from the belt at a more horizontal angle, either by various arrangements of straps or by a baldric, a broad strap hung from the right shoulder and running round the body across the left hip. One of the most common faults among actors and actresses wearing slung swords is the tendency to hold the weapon firmly by the grip in an attempt to stop it flapping around. The proper method is to allow the forearm or the hand to stay in light contact with the hilt between the weapon and the body. In this way the sword can be controlled by applying pressure to keep it lying close across the back of the hip or buttocks, especially if the performer wishes to make a bow without his sword coming into contact with those behind him. In the end it must be realized that, historically, people who wore swords at their sides had a different appreciation of their own and each other's personal space than we have in the modern world: today's performers and directors should make similar allowances.

The performers should ideally begin running through the fight in costume and/or armour as soon as these become available, so that any problems become apparent. If, as sometimes happens, an item of clothing or body protection causes problems which neither rehearsal nor a change in the choreography seems likely to eliminate, it will be necessary to approach the director and wardrobe person or costumier to see whether it can be altered or replaced. However, it is well worth spending a little time beforehand trying to work the problem through in rehearsal, as very often the performer will begin to feel easier after he has been given some time to 'wear in' his costume while practising the fight.

5 Character and Motivation

A good fight depends on the performers having a clear grasp of their characters' motivations. Therefore my system seeks to ensure that a production's fight choreography originates from the director's and performers' views of how the characters should react to the situations presented by the script, as well as my own. I think it sometimes surprises people that I should regard the performers' ability to move with and handle weapons in a co-ordinated manner as an intrinsic element of their work on the script, rather than solely an issue of health and safety. There are still some actors and directors who perceive that fight scenes are physical displays demanded by the script, during which a sort of generalized acted aggression can temporarily take the place of the surrounding drama's minutely observed characterization. I always try to persuade both parties that my input is intended to help extend the performers' physical and emotional ranges towards those of the characters as indicated by the script.

I believe all performers should strive just as hard to understand what compels their characters' behaviour during the fights as throughout every other passage in the script, otherwise they will have nothing on which to build a convincing portrayal. Choreography should not depend for effect on theatrical flourishes and I would rather choreograph a shorter routine, which when performed with energy and intention makes those watching believe in the characters' violent intentions, than a longer one during which the audience's sense of belief lapses.

When a fight director joins a production, he should first arrange to meet with the director and cast members who will appear in the fight scenes for a reading – or, if possible, a run-through. This will give them all an opportunity to discuss their views about the various participants' behaviour and motivation, so that a common agreement can be reached on how these factors cause the confrontation to develop. It is also the time to remind those present of the two cardinal rules: firstly, that the actors or actresses themselves must always be in total control of their actions; and secondly, that the audience should only ever believe the characters are in danger, never the performers themselves.

The fight director can then begin working with the cast, demonstrating the weapons and their appropriate fighting styles and encouraging each fighter to think through some of the possible moves open to his character. The emphasis should be on making each actor or actress aware of why one particular blow or body movement might be more effective than another. For example, is the character attacking because he believes his opponent is vulnerable, or because he himself is desperate? Is he defending confidently, drawing out his opponent, or has his nerve left him? Is he trying for a kill, or merely to wound or gain ground? Is the character in fact a good fighter, a bad or a lucky one? In the course of the fight do the fighters become weary but determined not to show it, or so weary that they cannot help showing it? Are they exultant or melancholy in victory? Angry or astonished in defeat? If the fight director can ensure this work continues throughout the training and rehearsal period in a positive atmosphere, everyone will feel involved in the shaping of the fight. Once a structure for the fight has emerged, all that remains is for it to be given a safe and aesthetic path around the set or location.

By way of a more detailed example, let us take a look at the final confrontation from Shakespeare's *Macbeth*, which has been played out many times both on stage and in screen adaptations, and consider how a fight director might choose to interpret the text. Staging fights for historical dramas from contemporary sources can be especially rewarding because the authors of these works and their audiences would have been familiar with the weapons they described, and therefore their characters' behaviour is likely to be relatively truthful. Playwrights like William Shakespeare and his contemporaries wrote sword-fighting scenes to be staged and performed by men for whom sword-practise was a common exercise. Moreover, since the need to put their training to the test in a real fight could arise at any time, many of the actors would have possessed that special level of fitness and alertness necessary for a fighter of any period. Just as importantly, their audiences would have been extremely critical of how far the reality in any combat scene was being stretched in the interests of dramatic licence.

The first thing to bear in mind is that both protagonists are hardened warriors. Yet Macbeth, for all his reputed ruthlessness, has in fact become increasingly guilt-ridden over the bloodshed resultant from his seizure of the throne, which includes the massacre of those closest to the man who will confront him in this scene: Macduff. Macbeth is aware, too, that part of the prophecy forecasting his own doom has already come to pass. Yet he fights on:

Why should I play the Roman fool and die
On mine own sword? Whiles I see lives, the gashes
Do better on them.

Macduff's:

Turn, hell-hound, turn!

is the cry of a man driven not only by a desire for retribution against the man responsible for the slaughter of his wife and children, but also seeking to absolve the guilt he himself feels over having left his family undefended against Macbeth's assassins.

Macbeth's reluctance to fight Macduff is immediately confirmed when he admits to his opponent,

> Of all men else I have avoided thee:
> But get thee back, my soul is too much charg'd
> With blood of thine already.

Macduff's reply:

> I have no words;
> My voice is in my sword: thou bloodier villain
> Than terms can give thee out!

make it plain that he is determined to see Macbeth dead at his feet.

What the characters should *not* do as the fight begins is rush at one another wildly and without control, either as characters or performers. Neither Macbeth's nor Macduff's years of battle training would have suddenly been forgotten, and neither should the performers' time working with the fight director. Instead, the nature of the action in this first section of the fight can be taken from Macbeth's warning to his opponent:

> Thou losest labour:
> As easy mayst thou the intrenchant air
> With thy keen sword impress as make me bleed.

This tells us that Macduff has expended a great deal of energy attacking without success, during which time Macbeth has refrained from killing him. Macbeth continues to try and warn Macduff off by declaring his supernaturally ordained invulnerability:

> Let fall thy blade on vulnerable crests;
> I bear a charmed life which must not yield
> To one of woman born.

But Macduff's retort reveals to him the deadly ambiguity of the witches' prophecy:

> Despair thy charm;
> And let the angel whom thou still hast serv'd
> Tell thee, Macduff was from his mother's womb
> Untimely ripp'd.

Macbeth curses the witches:

> That palter with us in a double sense;
> That keep the word of promise to our ear,
> And break it to our hope!

yet still he insists to Macduff: 'I'll not fight with thee!'
But Macduff, with no way of understanding his opponent's motives in seeking to avoid the challenge, taunts him:

> Then yield thee, coward,
> And live to be the show and gaze o' the time:
> We'll have thee, as our rarer monsters are,
> Painted upon a pole and underwrit
> 'Here may you see the tyrant.'

At this, Macbeth finally turns on him, for however Macbeth may be judged he is not a coward; he is a brave man faced with the realization of just how deeply he has allowed himself to be corrupted and dishonoured. He now determines that although Macduff has appeared as the embodiment of his doom, he will die fighting. He declares,

> I will not yield,
> To kiss the ground before young Malcolm's feet,

And to be baited with the rabble's curse.
Though Birnam Wood be come to Dunsinane,
And thou oppos'd, being of no woman born,
Yet I will try the last: before my body
I lay my warlike shield: lay on, Macduff;
And damn'd be him that first cries 'Hold, enough!'

It may now be agreed that the fight should become wild and savage, but it is up to both the fight director and the performers to ensure that the staging itself does not become uncontrolled. If the actors can bring to bear both their psychological and physical motivations, then the final section of the fight should give the impression of two mortal enemies at their most powerful and determined.

This fight is of course a classic example from a classic play, but the same analytical process should be carried out even for the most outlandish of characters or premises: only by fulfilling the demands of the script will the fight director's choreography inspire the performers and so convince and excite the audience.

PART TWO

Training – Keith Ducklin

6   Terminology

The fight sequences described and illustrated in this section form a comprehensive basis for training in medieval two-handed sword, medieval hand-and-a-half-sword (wearing armour), sixteenth-century single-handed sword and buckler, sixteenth- and seventeenth-century rapier and dagger, and late seventeenth-century transition rapier/eighteenth-century smallsword.

For this reason, each sequence incorporates a logically progressive range of techniques which, we believe, represents the fighting style of that particular weapon and period. As in many period manuals, the sequences are fought by a Master and his Scholar who have been given motivation but no specific characterization. The body mechanics of every movement are described and illustrated in detail, so that each technique can be carefully studied and followed by the reader who uses eye contact, balance and intent. The number and variety of techniques are by no means exhaustive, but are intended to form the basis for further study and experimentation. It is recommended that the section on body mechanics, from Part One of the book, be re-read in conjunction with the following section.

The descriptions are as far as possible free of historical and fencing terminology: this is because the nomenclature of sword techniques varies enormously between different historical periods and we believe the use of specific terms, however accurate, can cause unnecessary confusion even amongst experienced fighters. However, there are certain terms we will use to enhance the clarity of the descriptions and these are noted below.

The Sword

European swords are composed of four sections: blade; guard (to protect the hand); grip (the handle); and pommel (the counterweight to the blade). Guard, grip and pommel are collectively called the hilt. The blade itself then divides into five: the forte (roughly the third nearest the guard, where the blade is strongest), used wherever possible for blocking; the middle third, used for certain blocking actions, and also when applying pressure to bind, envelop or displace an opponent's blade; the foible (the third nearest the point), used for cutting and thrusting; the outside edge (the cutting edge, along the line of the sword-hand's fingers' middle knuckles) and the inside edge (sometimes used to parry in eighteenth-century smallsword fighting, along the line of the sword-hand's thumb knuckle).

The Body

When viewed as a series of targets, the human body is thought of as having clear divisions or lines of attack and defence: inside (to the left of a fighter's sword-arm); outside (to the right); high (above the fighter's waist); and low (below).

The Guards

These are the positions taken by the fighters at the beginning of the fight, from which they subsequently either attack or defend. Guards will be described according to which of the fighter's arms and feet are forward and which behind, together with the position, angulation and direction of their weapon or weapons.

Aiming Off and Pulling Blows

These are the two types of safety adjustment that can be made to each attacking blow's intent. Aiming off means that as the blow travels toward what in reality would be its target, its path is changed to another point away from the defender's body. A thrust to the stomach, for instance, would be aimed about ten inches to the left or right of the defender's body, depending on which side he decides to parry. When thrusting, the thumb of the sword- or dagger-hand guides the point to its target. Pulling a blow means arresting its movement as it travels toward what in reality would be its target, so that the weapon is stopped several inches short: the attacker's pulling point should be the same distance from the defender's body as his parrying point. A cut to the head, for instance, would be pulled about ten inches short. When cutting, the thumb guides the direction of the blow. When a cut is intended to miss, but in such a way that the follow-through (see Part One: Philosophy, Body Mechanics) takes the blade across the defender's body, the attacker must pull the blow just before full extension is reached, so that during the follow-through the blade can be safely drawn across and short of the defender's body whether or not he avoids. The attacker must always aim off or pull a blow and never believe that the defender will block as he is supposed to. The defender must never believe that the attacker will aim off or pull, and must defend or avoid as though the blow is being aimed with real intent.

In-distance and Out-of-distance Fighting

To attack and defend in-distance means that the fighters are close enough to hit each other if they do not adjust the level of intent of their attacks (see Part One: Philosophy, Body Mechanics). Out-of-distance means that they are sufficiently far away from each other that they cannot hit each other even when a cut or thrust is made with full intent. Generally speaking, cuts are made in-distance and pulled because they are powerful blows (often with heavier blades) and the fighters must not be over-balanced when delivering them. Thrusts can be made in- or out-of-distance and either pulled or aimed off. The choice of adjustment depends on the characteristics of the various sequences as well as the individual moves within them: in a rapier and dagger fight, where fighters mix cutting and thrusting attacks, the cuts should be made in-distance and pulled, therefore the thrusts must be in-distance too, and aimed off; in a smallsword routine, by comparison, there are a great many deeply committed lunges and very few cuts, so the majority of techniques will be most effectively made out-of-distance.

Types of Methods of Attack

When attacking, a cut is made with the edge of the blade, while a thrust is made with the point. Thrusts generally travel straight to their target (the volte, described later, is an exception), with either the fingers or the knuckles of the sword- or dagger-hand uppermost. Cuts have to be swung either in a half-circle (from the high to the low lines) or in full circle (from the low, through the high, and back to the low line again). The blade should never be swung out of the fighters' peripheral vision. Remember: for safety, all attacks must be either aimed off or pulled. If the fighters' blades are in contact in such a way that neither can break that contact without giving the other an opportunity to strike, the blades are said to be engaged. A glide is made when a fighter extends the blade continuously along and over the opponent's with a strong wrist action attempting to disarm the opponent or displace the opponent's blade. A bind is made when one fighter applies continuous blade pressure against another's intending to force the weapons into a different line. An envelopment is made when one fighter forces another's sword (and sometimes the hole of the sword-arm) over from one side of his body to the other. When making any attack, the sword must be travelling toward the target before the body moves (see Part One: Philosophy, Body Mechanics).

Types and Methods of Defence

The various defences with weapons, armour or clothing are often collectively called parries, but there is usually a distinction made between the block, which stops a cutting blow short of its target, and the beat which redirects the force of either a cut or thrust away from its target while leaving the defending weapon positioned for an immediate counter-attack. Blocks and parries should always be made with the edge of the blade, not the flat. Some parries travel straight across the body in the same line, while others travel either in a half-circle (from the high to the low lines) or in a full circle (from the low, through the high, and back to the low line again). Remember: the attack must always be defended as though it were being made with real intent – the defender should never assume that the attacker will safely adjust the blow. When defending the body should always move first, and the parry follow (see Part One: Philosophy, Body Mechanics).

Footwork

When moving the legs, a pass is a simple step forward or backwards where one foot passes the other. A side-step is a pass which carries the fighter's body sideways. A traverse is a side-step when one leg is thrown sideways but without passing the other. A lunge is a step forward or back with the leading leg alone, with the limb bent to bring the knee over the ankle, while the other leg is straightened. A volte is a specialized technique, described in greater detail in the eighteenth century smallsword sequence, which combines a sidestep with a thrusting attack. An avoidance is any combination of step, duck or jump when there is no attempt to block or beat parry the opponent's weapon.

7 Sequence One: Late Medieval Two-handed Sword

Special techniques

Our first sequence is fought entirely in-distance, with attacks either pulled or aimed off.

We will introduce the pass and sidestep, the glide to displace the opponent's blade, thrusting and pommelling to attack, and the diagonal sloping parry to defend.

Though the moves may seem simple enough, seeing them performed can quickly reveal to the trained eye a fighter's strengths and weaknesses. The principles explained here will form the groundwork for every other sequence.

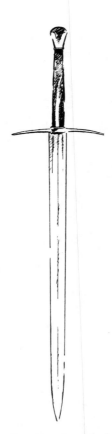

Fig. 1   The two-handed sword.

The weight of both fighters should be centred, their legs bent, feet as near as possible at right angles to each other, leaning neither forward nor back. There should be several inches between the heels, which should not be kept in line as is taught in modern fencing: rather the fighters should face square on to each other with both their upper and lower bodies, able to move with good balance either forwards, backwards or sideways as necessary.

Carriage

Fig. 2 Due to the sword's length, fighters appear to have generally carried two-handers in their hands or over their shoulders, without scabbards, rather than hanging them from the waist.

Grip

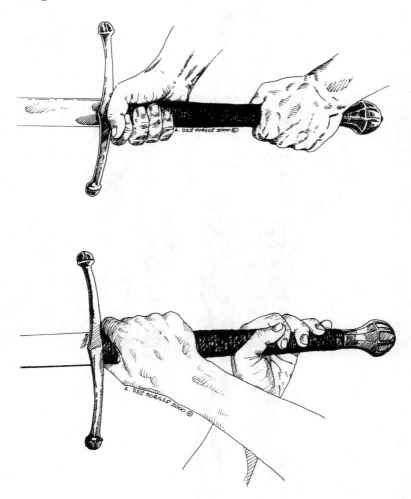

Fig. 3a & b The two-hander could be held with one hand just above the cross and the other near or on the pommel. Alternatively, leaving one hand on the grip, the other could grasp the blade – a useful technique when attacking at close quarters, or defending against heavy blows.

Fig. 4 The Master takes a guard with his sword held out in front, point aimed at his opponent's eyes, right leg forward.

The Scholar takes a guard with his sword to his high right, point aimed at his opponent's eyes, right leg back.

Fig. 5   The Scholar makes a cut for the Master's left leg just above the knee, swinging the sword in a clockwise half-circle, passing forward with his right leg. Remember: when attacking or defending, the fighters' sword-hands should never be out of their peripheral vision.

The Master side-steps to the right with his left leg, passing it in front of his right, beat parrying to his left, blade downwards.

Fig. 6   The Master then swings his sword from the beat in a clockwise circle to make a cut at the Scholar's left leg just above the knee, passing to his left and towards the Scholar by passing his right leg around his left.

The Scholar side-steps to the right with his left leg, passing it in front of his right, beat parrying to his left blade downwards, with the knuckles of his right hand up.

Fig. 7   The Scholar swings from the beat to cut down to the Master's head in a clockwise half-circle, passing to his left and towards the Master by bringing his right leg around his left. This cut is aimed off to the Master's left.

The Master's balance should now be centred in such a way that with his right leg forward the most natural direction for an evasion is to his right and with the left leg. This is the result of body mechanics at work: the type, target and direction of each attack, as well as the type and direction of the resulting defence, are always based on the options open to the fighters. When a move is made with correct balance and form, the most natural and useful options are immediately obvious. Options that arise from poor movement would in reality leave the fighter vulnerable, and theatrically, are unlikely to be constantly repeatable in performance because they have not resulted from an efficient use of the fighter's physicality.

The Master side-steps to the right with his left leg, passing it in front of his right, and makes a sloping parry by angulating his sword diagonally downwards, point to his rear, ensuring that the blade protects his head.

Fig. 8 When making a sloping parry, the defender should always be able to see the attacker framed in the area between the defender's blade and sword-arms.

Fig. 9   The Master cuts to the Scholar's left neck, passing to his left and towards the Scholar by bringing his right leg around his left.

The Scholar sidesteps by passing his left leg behind his right and parries to the left, blade upwards.

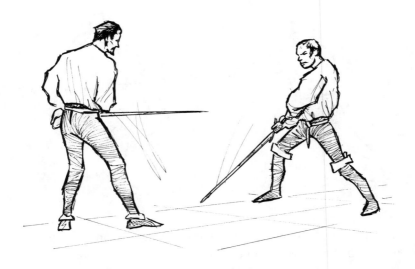

Fig. 10   The Scholar now displaces the Master's weapon to the Master's right with a glide against his opponent's sword. The Scholar should strongly extend his arms so that his blade glides along and over the length of his opponent's without loss of contact. The Scholar should increase the strength of the glide as he extends his arms, and at the end of the movement the Scholar's point should be directed towards the Master.

The Master, unable to resist the glide, allows his sword to be taken out of line to his right, saving his energy for the next defence. The glide is so swift that the Master has no chance to move, but instead can only wait to see his opponent's next intention.

Fig. 11   The Scholar thrusts at the Master's stomach, fingers up. He springs forward on the right leg rather than passing with the left, to deliver the attack more swiftly and directly. The thrust must be made by the Scholar first extending the arms, then stepping. The thrust is aimed off to the Master's right. Remember: when thrusting, the thumb guides the point.

The Master passes back with the right leg, bringing his blade over the Scholar's in an anticlockwise full circle and beat parries to the right, blade downwards.

Fig. 12   The Master uses the momentum created by the beat parry to keep his blade moving, swinging it in an anticlockwise full circle over and extending into a cut down at the Scholar's head, passing forward on the right leg.

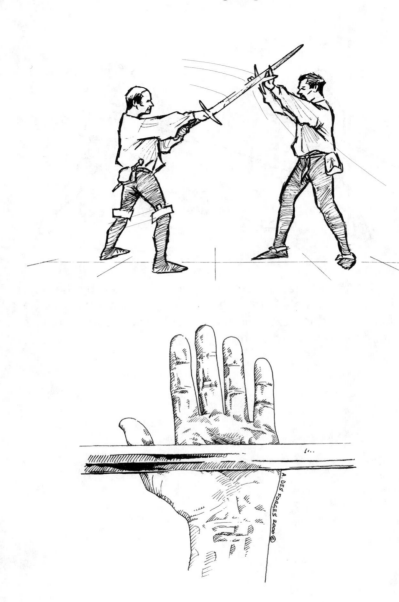

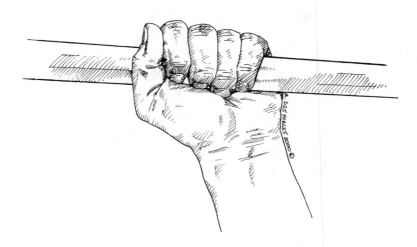

Fig. 13a, b & c   The Scholar does not pass back on the right leg but instead slips his left leg further back and blocks with his blade horizontal, point to the left, right hand on the grip, palm of the left hand on the blade a few inches from the top (this action can be made with the fingers open or closed – closed leaves them more vulnerable and is a grip better reserved for fighting in armour). The blade must be squarely positioned over the head so that in reality and theatrically the head is protected and there is no possibility of the fingers of either hand being struck. By not passing back, the Scholar has closed the distance between himself and his opponent.

Fig. 14   The Scholar beats the attacking blade to the Master's right using the cross. There is no foot movement on this action.

Fig. 15   The Scholar then attempts to strike the Master in the face with the pommel using a straight jab, right hand is still on the grip, the left on the blade, both hands knuckles up, springing forward on the right leg. This move is made in-distance, and the pommelling action aimed off to the left of the Master's face.

The Master traverses back and to the right on his right leg. Simultaneously he parries the Scholar's sword grip from right to left with his palm. He then closes his hand over the grip, immobilizing the weapon, and brings his own sword up, point aimed at the Scholar's stomach.

8 Sequence Two: Late Medieval Hand-and-a-half Sword

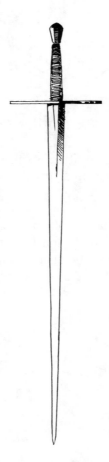

Fig. 16   The hand-and-a-half sword.

Special techniques

This sequence is fought entirely in-distance, with attacks either aimed off or pulled.

We will introduce two new types of attack, the axe-blow and the hook, during both of which the sword is held by the blade and the hilt used offensively. For the axe-blow the sword is swung and the cross used to deliver a bludgeoning blow; for the hook, the cross is used to pull the opponent's sword out of line.

The attacks and defences shown are based on those illustrated in a number of original fifteenth-century fight manuals, indicating that the armour worn in that period afforded the fighters the necessary manoeuvrability. Therefore, if the armour for a production has been chosen and fitted properly, the fighters should encounter no problems when making any of the attacks and defences shown.

Carriage

Fig. 17   The hand-and-a-half was short enough to be carried slung from the waist over the hip. A dagger was usually carried as a secondary weapon.

Grip

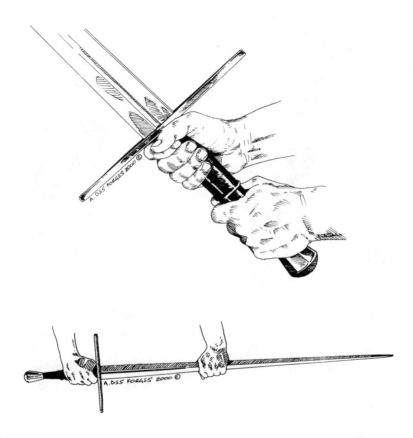

Fig. 18a & b   The hand-and-a-half was held in a similar fashion to the two-hander but, as described in Part One: Weapons Design, the shorter grip meant that if both hands rested on the grip, one was laid just above the cross and the other half on the grip and half on the pommel. Alternatively, by leaving one hand on the grip, the other could grasp the blade – a useful technique when attacking at close quarters, or defending against heavy blows.

Fig. 19   The Master takes a guard with his right leg back, sword resting with the blade back across his right hip, both hands on the grip.

The Scholar takes a guard with his right leg back, sword resting with the blade back over his right shoulder, both hands on the grip.

Fig. 20   The Scholar cuts to the left side of the Master's neck, passing forward with the right leg. Remember: the cut should be pulled just before full extension is reached so that during the follow-through the cut can be safely drawn across and short of the Master's body whether or not he avoids.

The Master avoids by passing back with his left leg and draws his sword across his body, bringing the point to face the Scholar.

Fig. 21   The Master thrusts at the Scholar's armpit, fingers up, not passing on the left leg but instead springing forward on the right. The thrust is aimed off to the Scholar's right.

The Scholar passes back on his right leg and beat parries blade downwards, detaching his left hand from the grip.

Fig. 22   The Scholar, having detached his left hand to give his right arm maximum mobility, uses the momentum from the beat parry to carry his sword in an anticlockwise diagonal circle over and down towards the right side of the Master's neck.

Fig. 23   As the Scholar's arm extends into the cut, he passes forward with his right leg.

The Master passes backwards with his left, parrying the Scholar's cut to the right, blade up.

Fig. 24   The Master then uses the cross of his sword to beat the Scholar's blade upwards. There is no foot movement at this point.

Sword Fighting

Fig. 25   The Master then swings his sword in a clockwise circle in reality upwards into the Scholar's groin, but theatrically aiming off to the Scholar's right.

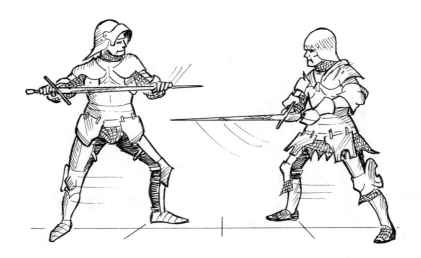

Fig. 26   As the Master's arms extend into the cut, he passes forward with the right leg.

The Scholar avoids by passing backward with his right leg, preparing to swing the hand-and-a-half in an axe-blow.

Holding the sword by the blade to attack with the hilt changes the weapon's balance: in reality the axe-blow would be an extremely powerful attack and this technique should be practised carefully until the fighter has developed the necessary control to pull the blow safely.

As the Scholar's right foot lands he begins by drawing back the sword so that the point momentarily threatens the Master.

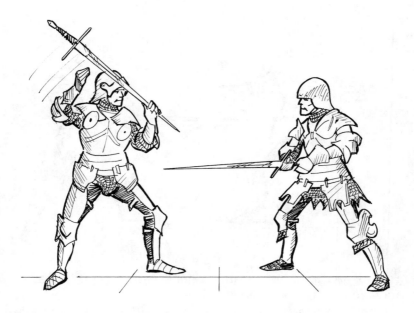

Fig. 27   His left hand then grasps the blade a few inches from the point and begins to swing it in an anticlockwise half-circle to make a stunning blow down to the master's head.

Fig. 28   At the same time he switches his right hand from the grip on to the blade so that both hands are now controlling the sword by the blade, attacking with the hilt. The preparation should run smoothly into the attack, and once the blade is travelling towards its target the Scholar passes forward with his right leg. The Master passes back a half-step only with his right, closing the distance between the fighters. To make the strongest possible defence, he blocks the axe-blow with his blade to the left, right hand on the grip, palm of the left hand on the blade a few inches along from the point.

Fig. 29   The Scholar should have extended sufficiently on this
attack to ensure that the master's block connects blade to blade
and not blade to grip. Realizing that the axe-blow has failed,
and the Master has closed the distance, the Scholar quickly pulls
his blade back and down to his left, using his cross as a hook in
an attempt to drag the master's blade out of line. The Scholar,
if he succeeds, can pommel the Master.

Fig. 30   The Master, to avoid being left vulnerable, releases his left hand from the blade as his weapon is pulled down and to his right. The lack of resistance causes the Scholar to retract his sword much further than he intended, giving the Master vital extra time to react to the following attack.

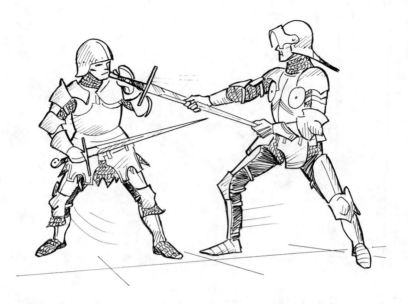

Fig. 31   The Scholar still attempts to pommel the Master in the face, springing forward with the right leg. The pommelling action is aimed several inches to the Master's right.

The Master side-steps back and to the left on his right leg. Simultaneously he parries the pommelling action to the right with his palm. He levels his sword at the Scholar's right armpit, in reality prepared if necessary to thrust as deeply as possible with the narrow point of the hand-and-a-half.

9 Sequence Three: Sixteenth-century Single-handed Sword and Buckler

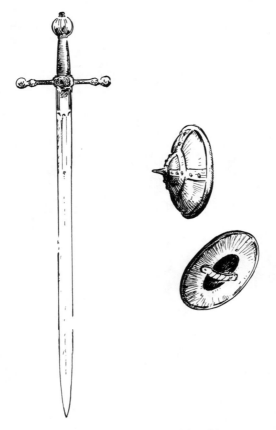

Fig. 32   The sword and buckler.

Special techniques

This sequence is fought entirely in-distance, with attacks either pulled or aimed off.

We will introduce the use of the buckler, which was used to beat aside an opponent's weapon or to deliver a punch to the opponent's body.

Carriage

Fig. 33 The sixteenth-century cross-hilt was worn slung from the waist over the hip. The buckler was generally hung over the sword, and if a man deliberately adopted a swaggering walk, or *swash*, his buckler would clatter noisily against his sword. This was the origin of the expression *swashbuckler*, which – despite its heroic connotations today – originally signified a rowdy individual or potential troublemaker.

Grip

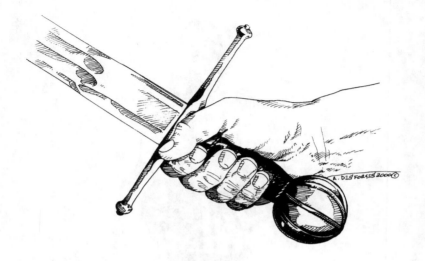

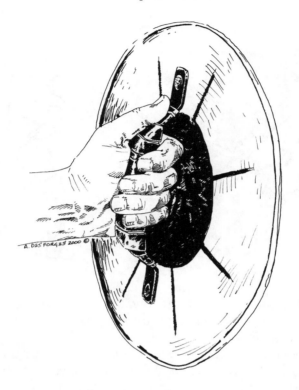

Fig. 34a & b   The sword, single-handed, just above the cross; the buckler either in a fist-grip or with the thumb behind.

Fig. 35   The Master takes a guard with his right leg back but his sword low and to the left, his buckler held out to cover his sword-hand, knuckles up.

The Scholar takes a guard with his right leg forward and his sword held out in front, his buckler held in line with the hilt of his sword. Neither fighter should allow the buckler to fall away from his body during either attack or defence.

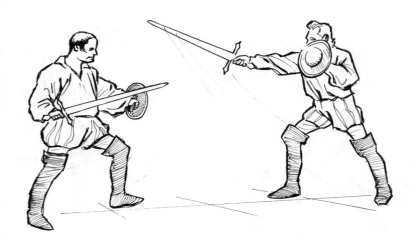

Fig. 36 The Master cuts diagonally upwards under the Scholar's wrists, allowing his sword-hand to turn from knuckles up to fingers up, passing forwards on the right leg. The Scholar avoids by passing back with his right leg without parrying.

Fig. 37   The Scholar thrusts at the Master's stomach, fingers up, passing forward with his right leg. The thrust is aimed off to the Master's left.

The Master steps back with his right leg and beat parries the attack away from his stomach to his left with his buckler.

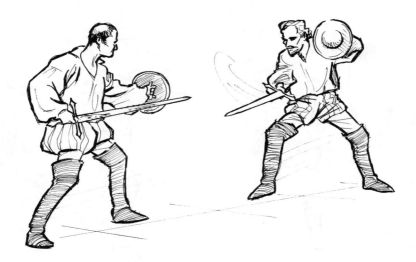

Fig. 38   The Master cuts across the Scholar's stomach, knuckles up, passing forward with his right leg. The cut is pulled to allow a safe follow-through.

The Scholar jumps back with his right leg.

Fig. 39   The Master immediately follows up the stomach cut with another cut, this time down to the Scholar's head, passing forward on the left leg. He aims this cut slightly off to the Scholar's right. The Scholar side-steps to his left, right leg across left, and takes a sloping parry, blade diagonally down and to the right.

Fig. 40a & b   The Scholar turns his sloping parry into a cut across the Master's stomach, knuckles up, passing round his right leg with his left. The cut is pulled to allow a safe follow-through.

The Master leaps back to land right leg back. As he leaps he raises both weapons high: this helps him jump back a good distance and land on balance. The action also ensures that his arms are not cut.

Fig. 41   The Master thrusts to the Scholar's stomach, fingers up, aiming off to the Scholar's left, passing with the right leg.

The Scholar side-steps to his right, left leg behind right, parrying blade downwards to his left. This movement closes the distance between the fighters.

Fig. 42   The Scholar aims a pommelling blow at the Master's face, knuckles up, springing forward on his right leg. The pommel should be aimed on but pulled short.

The Master passes back with his right leg and beats the pommel to his right with his buckler.

Fig. 43   The Master thrusts at the Scholar's stomach, fingers up, passing forward with his right leg. The thrust is aimed off to the Scholar's left.

   The Scholar passes back with his right leg, beating the attack away from his stomach to the left with his buckler.

Fig. 44   The Scholar thrusts at the Master's stomach, knuckles up, passing with his right. The thrust is aimed off to the Master's right. The Master traverses to his left and makes an anticlockwise circular parry with his sword over his opponent's blade to the right.

Fig. 45   The Master punches the Scholar in reality in the
kidneys, springing in on the left leg. Theatrically the punch must
be pulled, but this time light and controlled contact should be
made against the scholar's body in the areas of the latimus dorsi
muscles, which will absorb the blow safely.

The Scholar must however prepare himself to take the impact
of the punch without flinching. As he receives the blow he
arches his body back over the buckler to give the necessary
impression that a powerful blow has landed.

10 Sequence Four: Sixteenth & Seventeenth-century Rapier and Dagger

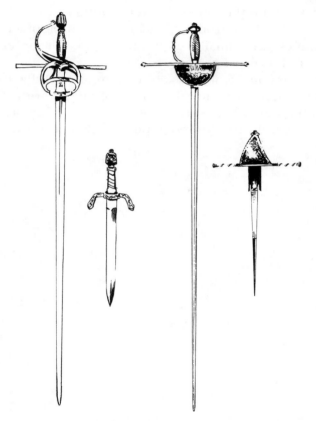

Fig. 46   The sixteenth-century swept-hilted rapier and dagger, *left*, and the seventeenth-century cup-hilt and dagger, *right*.

Special techniques

The moves of the following rapier and dagger sequence are made entirely in-distance, with attacks either pulled or aimed off.

During this sequence we will introduce the offensive and defensive use of the dagger in the left hand. We will also examine the technique of deliberately engaging an opponent's blade, during which one fighter maintains prolonged contact with his own weapon against his opponent's in order to limit the other fighter's options for attack or defence. We also introduce bind and the envelopment. The techniques are equally useful for swept-hilt or cup-hilt rapier and dagger fighting.

In this sequence, we will also explore more fully how the fighters might in reality deliver some attacks with greater intention than others as they try to gain the advantage, and how theatrically the choreography should convey this.

Carriage

Fig. 47   The rapier was worn with the scabbard in a hanger, suspended from a belt so that it hung over the left hip. The dagger was worn to the right.

Grip

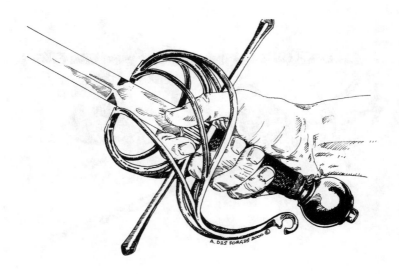

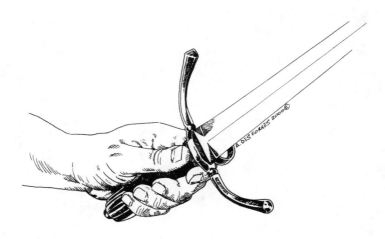

Fig. 48a & b   The rapier is held in a similar way to many Medieval and Renaissance cross-hilts, except for the difference that the forefinger is curled over the cross on the outside of the blade and back through the finger ring. If the dagger has a protective ring attached to the cross, it should be held with the ring protecting the knuckles and the thumb against the flat of the blade on the opposite side. It should *never* be held with the thumb passed through the ring!

Fig. 49a & b   The incorrect way to guide the sword when moving around and bowing. . . .

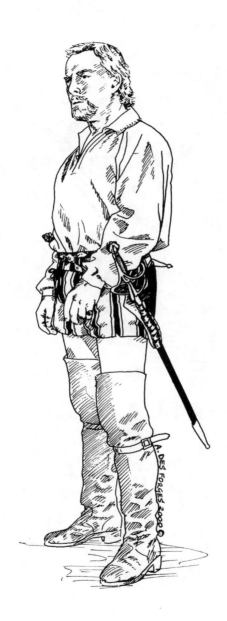

Fig. 50a & b   . . . And the correct way.

Fig. 51a & b   Drawing the rapier first, followed by the dagger. . . .

Fig. 52   . . . And falling into a guard.

Fig. 53   The Scholar takes a guard with his right foot and sword held in front, left foot and dagger drawn back so that the hilts of the rapier and dagger are level and in line. The knuckles of both hands face up.

The Master takes a guard with the right foot and rapier drawn back, the left foot and dagger held forward so that the points of both the rapier and dagger are level and in line. The knuckles of both hands are up.

Fig. 54   The Master makes the first attack with a deep and committed thrust to the Scholar's stomach between the Scholar's weapons, fingers up, passing forward with the right leg. The thrust is aimed off and to the Scholar's left. Remember: the thumb guides the direction of the thrust.

The Scholar steps back with the right leg, parrying with the dagger in a clockwise circular motion over the attacking blade and taking it to his left away from his stomach.

Fig. 55   The Scholar keeps the Master's rapier engaged with his dagger and thrusts to the Master's stomach between the Master's weapons, fingers up, passing forward with the right leg. The thrust is aimed off and to the Master's left.

The Master, realizing that his fully committed first thrust has left him vulnerable and that his rapier is still in contact with the Scholar's dagger, side-steps to the right with his left (rear) leg. If the Master's attack has been made properly and with good balance and full commitment, body mechanics will make the side-step easier and safer than passing straight backwards. As the Master side-steps he defends in a clockwise circle over the attacking blade taking it to his left away from his stomach.

Fig. 56   The Master keeps his dagger in contact with the Scholar's rapier and attempts to force the dagger around the outside of the rapier with a bind, in reality into the Scholar's face. Theatrically, the dagger should be aimed above the Scholar's head. There is no step at this point.

The Scholar opposes the pressure of the Master's dagger against his rapier with equal force.

The Master, realizing that his initial attack has been thwarted, takes advantage of the Scholar's vulnerable position to attempt a side-kick to the groin with his left leg, pivoting on his right. In preparation for the kick the knee should first be brought up and bent at waist level, so that the forward extension of the leg can be as precisely targeted and pulled as any sword thrust. The Master kicks, landing the sole of his foot firmly on the Scholar's upper thigh, the Master's leg three-quarters extended.

The Scholar, realizing that his groin is vulnerable, turns his body to the left (without stepping on either leg) so that his hip protects his groin, leaving both fighters momentarily balanced in this position. This move teaches both fighters to properly assess their distance as well as maintain balance.

Fig. 57 The Master then attempts, in reality, to kick the Scholar away and off balance by extending the left leg to its full length while keeping his balance centred over his right.

The Scholar, realizing the Master's intention, continues to keep eye contact with the Master over his right shoulder while turning even further to the left and passing his right leg back and around past his left to keep his balance.

Fig. 58   The Scholar's left foot lands as the upper half of his body completes a half-turn. After a moment's loss turning his head he now has eye contact with the Master over his left shoulder. His left foot and dagger face the Master, while his right leg and sword are drawn back. Throughout the whole turn the Scholar attempts to keep his weapons trained on the Master.

The Master shifts his balance off his right leg as the Scholar absorbs the kick, allowing his own left leg to fall forwards.

Fig. 59 The Master, judging the distance that now exists between himself and the Scholar and seeing that the Scholar is recovering his balance after the turn, makes a cut down to the Scholar's head, passing forward with the right leg. (A thrust to the face would be a more likely attack at this point, but these types of attacks carry a high level of risk even for skilled practitioners and are not demonstrated in this book.) This head cut would in reality be a strong and committed one in order to force the Scholar to block with both sword and dagger, but theatrically this power must be suggested by the performer's ability as an actor – the blow must be safely pulled. Also, in reality and theatrically, if the Master steps in too deeply with his attack he will leave himself vulnerable, therefore his judgement of distance must be such that he is able to finish the attack with no more than six inches of blade over the Scholar's head, no matter how near or far away the Scholar lands.

The Scholar, realizing the power of the cut, passes back with his left leg and blocks with the sword and dagger crossed. Because the left leg leads the retreat, the dagger will rise first and under it the sword.

Fig. 60   The Master immediately follows up with a dagger thrust to the stomach, fingers up, passing with the left leg. The thrust is aimed on target but pulled several inches short of the Scholar's body with the arm fully extended. As the thrust reaches its full extension, the Master draws back his rapier to prepare for the next attack.

The Scholar, feeling the withdrawal of the Master's rapier, passes back on his right leg and drops both sword and dagger, still crossed, to block the dagger thrust.

Fig. 61   The Master presses with a third consecutive attack by cutting diagonally upwards, in reality at the exposed left side of the Scholar's neck, but theatrically several inches above the head so that it will miss even if the Scholar does not make the necessary following move. Because of the proximity of the fighters at this point there is no reason for the Master to step forward on the attack, so he generates the necessary power with his upper body.

The Scholar ducks back and slightly to the right, throwing his right leg back under him to enable him to drop as low as possible while still keeping good balance. As he does so he draws back his rapier and extends his dagger.

Fig. 62   The Scholar sees the Master's upward cut reach its full extension and thrusts at the Master's stomach from his low position, knuckles up, passing on the right leg. The thrust is aimed off to the Master's right.

The Master passes back and to the left on his left leg, allowing the rapier to drop under its own weight in an anticlockwise circular movement, beat parrying the Scholar's attack to the Master's right. Simultaneously, he changes the dagger from the conventional upward grip to a downward one.

Fig. 63 The Master keeps the Scholar's rapier engaged with his own and stabs downward with his dagger at the Scholar, aiming in reality for the right side of the Scholar's neck, but theatrically past the right shoulder with the dagger point turned away to the Scholar's right, passing forward with his left leg.

Fig. 64   The Scholar leaps forward and sideways on his left leg
to avoid the downward stab.

Fig. 65   The Master draws back the dagger and slashes from left to right across the Scholar's back, passing on the left leg. As with sword cuts which are to be avoided, the dagger slash must be pulled just before full extension so that the blow can be safely followed through even if the Scholar does not move.

The Scholar avoids the slash, jumping back with both hands in the air for safety, to land with his right leg behind, sword drawn back. Remember: jumping with the hands in the air allows greater distance to be made and saves the arms from being cut.

Fig. 66   The Scholar fully commits to a thrust at the Master's stomach, fingers up, passing forward with the right leg. The thrust should be aimed off to the Master's left.

The Master side-steps to the right, passing with the left leg in front of the right, and parries with the dagger over and clockwise to the left.

Fig. 67   The Master attacks with a thrust to the Scholar's stomach, fingers up, passing forward with the right leg. The thrust should be aimed off and to the Scholar's left

The Scholar side-steps to the right with his left leg behind his right, parrying over and clockwise to the left with his dagger.

Fig. 68   The Scholar immediately uses his dagger to envelop the Master's rapier in a high clockwise full-circle over to the Master's left, passing forward with his left leg. In reality and theatrically, the Master keeps his rapier engaged throughout the bind because he is gauging the Scholar's intentions. Both Master and Scholar must take care that they do not allow the weapons to become disengaged, or cross level with the Master's face, during this envelopment.

The Scholar completes the envelopment and at the same time attempts in reality to barge the Master off balance as he passes forward on his left leg, making contact with his upper left arm against the Master's right. Theatrically, contact should be made in the same controlled fashion as the kick in the earlier part of the sequence, teaching both fighters the necessary awareness to ensure that neither actually loses his balance.

Fig. 69   The Master braces himself for the impact and opposes it with equal energy, using that energy in a positive way to bounce himself away and make distance. The Master lands still facing the Scholar with his right shoulder.

Fig. 70   The Scholar makes a downward cut to the Master's head with his rapier, passing forward with the right leg, but this cut is not fully committed as it is designed to draw the Master out. The Master passes back with the right leg and raises his dagger alone, point to the right, to block.

Fig. 71   The Master makes a thrust with his rapier at the
Scholar's stomach, knuckles up, passing forward with the right
leg. The thrust should be aimed off to the Scholar's right.

The Scholar passes back with the right leg, allowing the
rapier to drop in an anticlockwise half-circle, beat parrying the
Master's rapier to the right.

Fig. 72   The Scholar then allows his own sword's momentum to carry it anticlockwise back and over into a downward cut to the Master's head, passing forward with his right leg. This time the cut is in reality a heavy one, though theatrically it must be safely pulled.

The Master passes back on his right, but realizing that he has to protect himself from a heavy blow, blocks with both sword and dagger. As the right foot is retreating, the sword will rise first, and under it the dagger.

Fig. 73 The Scholar continues the attack, thrusting to the Master's stomach with his dagger, knuckles up, passing forward with the left foot. The thrust should be aimed off to the Master's left. The Scholar does not withdraw his rapier as he thrusts.

The Master, sensing the continued engagement of the Scholar's rapier on his own, side-steps to his right with his left leg in front of his right and parries clockwise with his dagger alone, taking the Scholar's rapier to the Scholar's left. The Master simultaneously applies pressure to the Scholar's rapier, pushing it to the Scholar's right.

Fig. 74   If the three actions of step, parry and push are carried
out by both fighters with correct timing, the Scholar's body will
be wrenched to his right.

Fig. 75   The Master then raises his left foot against the back of the Scholar's left knee intending to force the Scholar's leg to the floor with a push. In reality, this would cause the Scholar to fall heavily on the knee, but theatrically the push should be delivered with control, the Master keeping balanced over his right leg.

Fig. 76   The Scholar is forced to the ground, but both in reality and theatrically he controls his own fall by turning his body
to the right and allowing the left leg to slide under him so that
the knee does not take the impact.

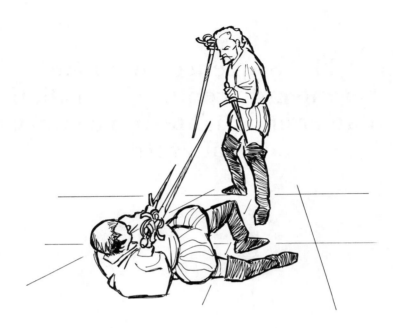

Fig. 77   As he makes his escaping movement he also tries to put as much distance as he can between himself and the Master. He finishes on his back, facing the Master, prepared to defend himself as best he can.

11   Sequence Five: Late Seventeenth-century Transition Rapier and Eighteenth-century Smallsword

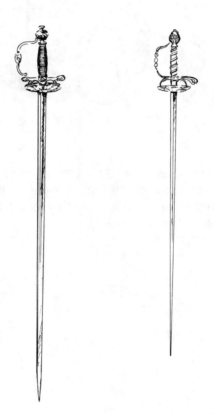

Fig. 78   The transition rapier, left, and smallsword, right.

Special techniques

The majority of techniques used when training and fighting with these weapons were thrusting ones and therefore the moves in this sequence are largely aimed on target but out-of-distance. There are however some techniques performed in-distance, which are so noted in the text.

For our last sequence, we will introduce the techniques of attacking and defending while keeping the right leg advanced, including the lunge and recovery, and the volte.

Carriage

Fig. 79 & 80 (*left*)   Both weapons were carried over the left hip, either slung from the waist, or hung from a baldric, a broad strap running diagonally over the right shoulder and down across to the left side. During the late seventeenth and early eighteenth century, belts and baldrics were often worn over the waistcoat, whereas by the late eighteenth century they were more usually worn beneath.

Grip

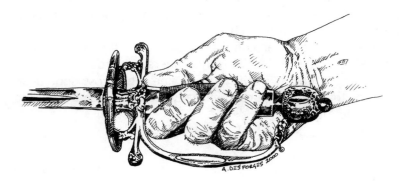

Fig. 81   The earlier transition rapier with its heavier blade often retained finger rings below the cross, so that it could be held like the old style swept-hilt for greater control. The smallsword, with its lightweight and easily manoeuvrable blade, often had finger rings which were purely decorative, and the sword was held by the grip between the index finger and thumb.

The basic fighting stance in transition rapier/smallsword is with the legs rather more narrowly aligned than in earlier periods, though not necessarily with the heels exactly in line as is commonly taught in modern fencing. The right leg is advanced about eighteen inches from the left (though this distance will vary according to the individual fighter's physique) and both are comfortably bent so that the fighters' bodies are centred and their weight evenly distributed. Both fighters' upper bodies should be square on to the opponent.

The sword-arm should be held out from the body, the elbow about a hand's span in front of and in line with the ribs. In this position the sword-arm is flexed at the elbow, able to extend into an attack or retract into a defence. When on guard the fighters' swords' point should be trained on their opponent's eyes. The left arm should be held reasonably high and to the left of the face, so it can just be seen with the fighter's peripheral vision, though the exact position varied according to the individual masters' teachings.

Though the techniques in this fight are applicable to both transition rapier and smallsword, the illustrations show the fighters dressed as Master and Scholar from a late eighteenth century salle, or fencing school.

Master and Scholar come on guard with the swords positioned from right to left with the fingers upwards, so that the blades are engaged in the outside line. The cross should be made so that the points can be clearly seen between the eyeline of the two fighters.

Fig. 82   In reality, if the fighters came on guard they would do so at a distance close enough to allow them to hit each other with their lunges.

Fig. 83   Theatrically, both fighters must be capable of making even a fully extended lunge from this guard while keeping out-of-distance and there should be no more than three inches of sword above the cross.

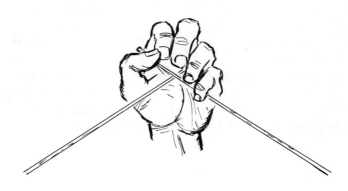

Fig. 84   A good technique is for the fight director to try and close his hand over the points above the cross: if he can do so, the fighters are at a good distance.

Fig. 85   This engagement of blades means that neither fighter can hit his opponent with a straight thrust to the outside line. An option which overcomes the stalemate is for one of the fighters to disengage his blade from the outside line and attack instead on the inside line. Since engagements and disengagements figure prominently in late seventeenth-, eighteenth- and early nineteenth-century sword-fighting, this is how the master will begin the fight

The Master disengages by allowing his point to drop from the engaged position under and slightly to the right of his opponent's sword, fingers upwards. There should be no reason for the elbow to be withdrawn during the disengagement.

Fig. 86   The Master then fully extends his arm so that the point is aimed directly at the centre of his opponent's right breast on the high inside line, thumb still upwards. *There is no other body or foot movement up to this point.* Only when the disengagement and extension have been made can the lunge forward be made. When a fight is performed at speed these separate movements will blur into one, but mastering the progression is *essential* for safety and accuracy of blade work: disengage first, then extend directly towards the target with the arm and sword, then lunge.

Fig. 87   The Master now makes the first lunge. This is in reality an exploratory attack and not fully committed, but both in
reality and theatrically it must carry the Master sufficiently far
forward to provoke a reaction from the Scholar. Keeping the
sword-arm and blade on target and fully extended, the master
kicks forward with the right foot. The sole of the left foot
remains flat on the ground as the rest of the leg straightens,
while the right leg lands with the knee directly over the ankle.

The left foot should never roll forward so that the ankle rubs
the floor, and the right knee should never roll forward over the
ankle. In reality and theatrically both these actions can damage
the knees. Also, they result from a potentially dangerous over-
commitment, because if the fighter must first rock back the
right knee and roll back the left foot to bring the body out of
the lunge, he is wasting a precious split second which might
cost him dearly. The upper body should not be thrown towards
the opponent but remain centred, having been carried as far
forward as necessary by the lunge. The sword-arm should never
need to be retracted during the lunge: if at any time the fighters extend their blades and realize they are closer than they
should be, they should keep the arm and sword extended and
shorten the length of their lunge.

The Scholar raises his right foot slightly from the ground and takes a half-step back, keeping the right foot forward but reducing the distance between the feet to between ten and twelve inches. This movement must be a *step*, and not a drag of the foot along the floor. He parries the Master's thrust to the left with the fingers upwards, point up, leaving the blade trained from left to right on his opponent's eyes.

Fig. 88   The Scholar immediately extends his blade (which is already on the inside of the Master's, so obviating the need for any further disengagement) towards the centre of the Master's chest and makes an identical exploratory lunge.

The Master recovers, or brings back his body from the lunge position by bending his left knee and bringing back his right foot to leave both feet once again about eighteen inches apart. As he recovers he parries as described above. The recovery should always be made in the legs, and not by throwing back the upper body. Two more chest lunges and parries are exchanged on the right legs, so that the Master is in receipt of the final lunge.

Fig. 89a & b The Master now changes tactics, and glides the Scholar's blade to his left to open up his outside line. Remember: applied with a strong wrist action, turning the sword-hand from thumb upwards to knuckles upwards, this gliding action would in reality not only displace the Scholar's blade to his left but quite possibly disarm him. Theatrically, therefore, care must be taken that only enough force is applied to take the Scholar's blade out of line (unless a disarm is choreographed). The glide leaves the Master's point aimed at the Scholar's stomach. The Scholar in reality retains his grip on the sword, and theatrically allows his blade to be carried out of line without losing control of it.

Fig. 90   The Master, his sword at full extension towards the Scholar's stomach, now makes a deep and fully committed lunge, knuckles up. To preserve balance and line, he throws back his left arm at the same time, also knuckles up, and lunges on the right leg.

The Scholar, under pressure, makes a passing step back on the right leg, parrying blade downwards to the right with the knuckles up, drawing the Master as deep into his attack as possible.

Fig. 91   The Scholar immediately fully commits to a volte by extending towards the Master's right hip, hand moving from knuckles up to fingers up, and passing forward and sideways to the Master's right on his right leg. The right foot should point on the same direction as the sword blade. As he does so the Scholar throws back his left arm, fingers up, to allow him to arch his body as far as possible out of line. This throwing back of the left arm ensures that the Scholar's body mechanics keep the sword's point on target and prevent what should be a thrust becoming a slap with the side of the blade.

The Master fully extended, quickly recovers by passing back on the right leg, parrying blade downwards to the right with the knuckles up, drawing the Scholar as deep into the volte as possible.

Fig. 92   The Master begins a bind, raising the Scholar's sword in an anticlockwise motion intending in reality a thrust to the inside line if the Scholar does not oppose him. Theatrically, the point of the Master's sword must be raised over the Scholar's head, so that the point never comes near his face. He does not get the opportunity to thrust however, so there is no foot movement at this point.

The Scholar, aware of the Master's intention, opposes with equal force, keeping his blade engaged with the Master's to forestall any attempt at a thrust.

Fig. 93   The Master realizes that the Scholar is preventing the intended attack, and instead turns the bind into an envelopment, taking the Scholar's blade over his head while stepping forward on his right leg to displace the Scholar's blade to the Scholar's right, throwing him off balance.

The Scholar passes back on his right leg as soon as he feels the Master's change of intention. The Scholar refuses to let his blade be thrown aside and keeps it engaged with the Master's, turning his knuckles up so that the envelopment finishes with the Master's blade under the guard of the Scholar's sword, which points straight down.

Fig. 94   The Master continues to attack by swiftly drawing back his blade low and to the left and attempting, in reality, a right-to-left upward diagonal slash across the Scholar's right neck, knuckles upwards. Theatrically, the cut should be aimed several inches away to the right of the Scholar's right cheek and past his head, so that he cannot be struck even if he fails to make the necessary following move.

The Scholar, still facing the Master, throws himself back, straightening the left leg and bending the right. At the same time he ducks as low as possible, drawing back his sword, knuckles upwards. In reality, this move allows him to avoid the slash as well as giving him room to aim his weapon.

Fig. 95   The Scholar sees the Master's upward cut reach its full extension and thrusts at his stomach, passing forward with his right leg. Because the fighters are still close, this thrust is made in-distance, aimed off to the Master's left, thumb on top. Because the passing actions of the previous few moves will have brought the fighters closer together, this thrust should be aimed off to the Master's left.

The Master removes his body by stepping to the right with his left leg behind his right, parrying to his left, blade down, knuckles up.

Fig. 96   The Master attempts to pummel the Scholar in the face but theatrically pulls the blow by several inches, springing forward on the right leg.

The Scholar jumps back on the right leg, simultaneously opening the palm of his left hand to slap the Master's extended sword-hand aside to his right. Both fighters break off.

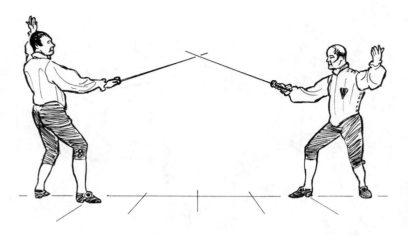

Fig. 97   Both fighters come into their original guard again. As
before, neither fighter can expect to make a successful attack
without breaking the engagement.

Fig. 98   The Master disengages. . . .

Fig. 99   . . . extends towards the Scholar's chest. . . .

Fig. 100   . . . and makes a committed lunge, fingers up, left arm thrown back palm up, on the right leg.

The Scholar immediately retreats, stepping back first not with his right leg but with his left leg. The right leg remains bent. As he moves back, the Scholar brings the point of his blade back on line towards the Master. Both fighters' feet land together.

The timing of this sequence is all-important. The test for the fighters should be to make sure they are moving in perfect co-ordination, otherwise, both in reality and theatrically, one or other would be at a disadvantage.

Fig. 101   The Master is aware that just as his right foot is land-ing, not only is the Scholar's left foot doing the same, but his right is also beginning to retreat. The Master therefore brings up his left foot so that, again, both fighters' feet land together.

The Scholar, as he steps back on his right, makes a clockwise circular parry under the Master's blade, and brings his own blade upward and to the right as he turns the parry, fingers up, into an engagement.

The Master, feeling the Scholar engaging his blade, engages the Scholar's, bringing them both back into their previous guard position, swords held right to left, fingers up. The Master presses the Scholar by disengaging a second time to the inside line, extending and lunging on the right leg, this time without full commitment.

The Scholar retreats and parries in the same way, bringing them back to the guard once again.

Fig. 102 The Master makes a third lunge on the right leg. He has not fully committed to the lunge and is giving the Scholar the opportunity to regain the advantage.

The Scholar parries in the same circular fashion, this time with his blade up but closing off the outside line with the knuckles up.

Fig. 103 The Scholar immediately glides the Master's blade to the Master's left.

Fig. 104   The Scholar then extends towards his stomach and thrusts, fingers up, lunging on the right leg.

The Master recovers from his lunge with a passing step back, parrying to the right, knuckles up.

Fig. 105   The Master extends towards the Scholar's stomach and thrusts, fingers up, lunging on the right leg.

The Scholar recovers from his lunge with a passing step back, parrying to the right, knuckles up.

Fig. 106 The Scholar begins to envelop the Master's sword. There is no foot movement at this point.

The Master opposes with equal force, also with no foot movement.

Fig. 107   As the envelopment reaches the point where the swords are safely over both fighters' heads, the Scholar sidesteps forward and to his left attempting to change the direction of his attack.

The Master, realizing the Scholar's intention, steps forward and out on his left to preserve the fighting distance, keeping contact with the Scholar's blade.

Fig. 108   At this point both fighters understand that neither can gain any advantage and both break away in the directions they are already moving, maintaining the envelopment until the last moment.

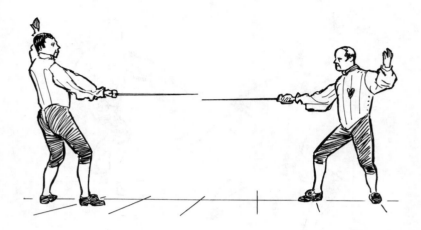

Fig. 109   For the final section, both fighters come into an open guard, blades forward right to left, fingers up, but with no engagement. Theatrically, both Scholar and Master should now be aware enough to ensure that the distance between them is adequate to permit extensions and lunges without risk of contact.

Fig. 110 The Scholar extends and thrusts to the Master's chest, fingers up, lunging with the right leg.

The Master recovers a half-step on the right leg and parries to his left, blade upwards, fingers up.

Fig. 111 The Master extends and thrusts to the chest, fingers up, lunging with the right leg.

The Scholar recovers from his lunge and parries to his left, blade upwards, fingers up.

Fig. 112 The Scholar extends and thrusts to the stomach, fingers up, lunging with the right leg.

The Master recovers from his lunge and parries blade downwards to the left, knuckles up.

Fig. 113 The Master extends and thrusts to the stomach, knuckles up, lunging with the right leg.

The Scholar recovers from his lunge and parries blade downwards to the left, knuckles up.

Fig. 114   The Scholar extends and thrusts to the Master's chest, knuckles up, lunging with the right leg.

The Master recovers from his lunge and parries to the left, blade upwards, fingers up.

Fig. 115   The Master extends and thrusts to the Scholar's chest, fingers up, lunging with the right leg.

The Scholar recovers from his lunge and parries to the left, blade upwards, fingers up.

Fig. 116 The Scholar extends and thrusts to the Master's chest, fingers up, lunging with the right leg.

The Master recovers from his lunge and parries to the left, blade upwards, fingers up.

Fig. 117 The Master immediately glides the Scholar's sword to the Scholar's left.

Fig. 118   The Master thrusts to the Scholar's stomach, fingers up, lunging with the right leg.

The Scholar retreats with both legs, parrying to the right, blade downward, knuckles up. The Master pursues him, bringing up his left leg as the Scholar steps back with his right.

Fig. 119   The Master disengages to the inside line, using is wrist to flip the point *over* the Scholar's blade.

Fig. 120   The Master then extends and thrusts to the Scholar's stomach, fingers up, lunging with the right leg.

The Scholar retreats with both legs, parrying blade down to the left, knuckles up. The Master brings up his left foot as the Scholar steps back on his right.

Fig. 121   The Scholar, having retreated twice under pressure, regains the advantage by swiftly thrusting to the Master's stomach, knuckles up, lunging with the right leg. The Master retreats on the left foot.

Fig. 122   The Master completes a circular parry over and to his right, blade down, knuckles up, bringing back his right foot.

The Scholar pursues him, bringing up his left leg as the Master steps back on his right.

Fig. 123   The Scholar disengages over to the inside line and the previous attack and defence are repeated.

Fig. 124   The Scholar disengages over a third time and attacks, but this time fully commits to the lunge, throwing his left arm back knuckles up, and does not prepare to bring up the left leg.

The Master retreats with a pass on the right leg, drawing the Scholar as deeply as possible into his lunge, and parries to the right, blade down, knuckles up.

Fig. 125   The Master attempts to extend and thrust beneath the Scholar's blade and under his ribs while keeping both blades in contact, knuckles up. The Master will finish the thrust with his sword-hand lower than his point.

The Scholar steps back on his right, parrying to the right, blade downwards, knuckles up.

Fig. 126   The Scholar attempts an identical attack.

The Master, instead of retreating, steps forward and to the left with his left leg, simultaneously redirecting the Scholar's bade to the Master's right by parrying blade downwards, knuckles up. As the Master's left foot lands, he grasps the Scholar's sword-hand and hilt with his left hand.

Fig. 127 The Master then takes the Scholar's sword-arm out of line in a circular motion from the Scholar's left to right, bringing his blade level with the Scholar's stomach.

12   Blocking the Fight

Blocking is the term often used in theatre, film and television to describe the pattern of each performer's movement and position throughout any given scene. For the first director, blocking is not necessarily exactly the same thing as choreography.

When the audience watches a performance on stage or screen they should be seeing a performer playing a character with a purpose, in pursuit of which the performer/character may carry out any number of movements and activities. One of the functions of the rehearsal period is for the performer and director to work together in defining a path around the stage, set, or location which will allow the performer not only to move and act truthfully, but also to create an interesting and, where necessary, exciting visual image for the audiences who eventually watch the production. If more characters become part of the scene, each moving in different ways for their own reasons, the accuracy of each performer's blocking becomes more crucial. If some or all of these people have to fight, their relative positions become absolutely critical.

To detail every aspect of how the moves of a fight might be blocked could fill a separate book. However, there are certain basics that should be noted. For ease of explanation we will use the standard theatrical terms of upstage, centre-stage and downstage, stage-right and stage-left, (which, for the uninitiated, describe the performers' positions *from their own point of view*).

The most important concern is safety. Obviously, the choreography and blocking should *never* carry the fighters so near the audience or film crew that these people are endangered. A technique like the glide, which in reality can disarm an opponent, may accidentally do so theatrically; a beat parry may knock the attacker's sword from his hand. If the fighters have been properly trained the chances of such accidents is minimal, but the fight director should ensure that these types of move are blocked in such a way that if the worst happens, the path of an uncontrolled weapon is towards a part of the stage, set or location unoccupied by any of the cast, crew or audience. If there is no way of ensuring this, such moves should not be choreographed. If a fight sequence includes a choreographed disarm, the same considerations should apply.

A fight director may choreograph a safe, truthful and logical set of moves, but if poor positioning means the fighters' body shapes are obscured from the audience or camera, or the safety adjustments made too obvious, then again the blocking must be thought through. Ideally, the choreography and blocking should be considered together, so that while each attack and defence arises from body mechanics, weapon design, clothing and character motivation, an exciting passage around the stage, set or location is also being planned.

The advantage with many in-distance attacks is that the fighters can be blocked to face each other in profile to the audience while still maintaining the illusion that, had the defender not parried successfully, in reality the cut or thrust would have landed. The exceptions are cutting attacks intended theatrically to miss because of an avoidance by the defender: these should be staged at between 45° and 90° to the audience, in order that when the cut is pulled during the follow-through this safety adjustment is less obvious.

As an example, our sixteenth-century rapier and dagger sequence, if choreographed straight from this book behind a proscenium arch (i.e. with the audience all in front), should begin with both fighters centre-stage in profile, the Master stage-right. The fight continues in profile as far as the kick off. During the Master's subsequent head cut and dagger thrust to the stomach, however, both Master and Scholar should bring themselves around to 45°, the kick forcing the Scholar back and upstage-left, so that the Master's cut up at the Scholar's neck is made with the blade between the Scholar and the audience. To the audience, the blow will appear to miss the Scholar by only a fraction as the performer ducks.

By comparison, out-of-distance fighting should be staged at a more acute angle because the majority of techniques are thrusts, which though aimed on target, reach their maximum extension well short of the defender's body. To block an out-of-distance thrust in profile will leave this safety adjustment in plain sight of the audience.

A good angle for this style of fighting is at between 45° and 60° to the audience, so that the audience can see the point apparently travelling to its target, while being less aware of the extra distance the fighters are giving themselves. Our smallsword sequence might therefore begin with the Scholar downstage-right, the Master upstage-left. In the first sequence, the Master's upwards cut to the Scholar's neck would then be made upstage, creating a better illusion, while the Scholar's palm slap against the Master's pommelling action would be aimed safely in the same direction.

Killing or wounding blows should be blocked to highlight either the reaction of the killer or victim, whichever has the more dramatic resonance. The acting skill of the performer playing the victim is particularly important if the audience is to get a realistic impression of both the physical and mental effects resulting from the final blow. For film and television, of course, there is the advantage of having special effects experts, editors, and lately computer wizards who can be called upon to create all sorts of gory injuries!

13 The Fight During Performance

In television or film, the fight director (or the stunt arranger who has directed the fights) is usually present for the whole period from the beginning of the performers' training through until the action scenes are 'in the can'. In the theatre, by contrast, it is often assumed that once the initial training and rehearsal period has come to an end the fight director's job is done: from then on it falls to those directly involved in the production to keep the action scenes safe and exciting. This might be regarded as a questionable approach, regardless of how much effort has gone into the planning of the fight scenes or how conscientiously those involved have trained – especially in an action-filled play. While it is true that the fight director cannot follow a play through every performance or visit it at every different venue, the production's director should ensure that the expert in whom they have placed their trust is recalled every so often to ensure that the fights are still being carried out safely and effectively.

For the duration of the run, it is now normal practice for the fight director to try and appoint a fight captain, a member of the cast with good fighting skills to keep an eye on the action and liaise with the production staff in case of any problems. This job should include: scheduling regular fight rehearsals with the cast (making sure the fighters are keeping their eye contact, balance, and attacking and defending with the correct level of intent); liaising with stage management to ensure proper maintenance of the weapons and the stage surface; reporting to wardrobe when the fighters' footwear is in need of repair; and ensuring that the first-aid box is always fully stocked and accessible – just in case. However, the fight captain should never allow himself to become involved in re-blocking the fight or training new cast members: these tasks are the province of the fight director.

In the end, of course, the most important factor in determining how effectively any fight continues to be performed is likely to be the same as that which governs the rest of the production: do the fighters believe what they are doing and acknowledge the fight moves as the logical physical embodiment of their characters' actions at that point in the play? Or, to end this book as we began it, has *reality* come *first*?

Afterword

No one is likely to become either proficient or safe in the use of historical or stage weapons by taking lessons solely from a book – even one as detailed as *Sword Fighting: a Manual for Actors and Directors.* Nevertheless, the reader who is new to the subject may have found in this book's text and illustrations a good basis for future study, while the established actor, director, fight director or martial artist may benefit from experimenting with some or all of John Waller's theories.

Let us end with one final quote from the Waller canon: 'When the attention of an audience is not on the choreography of the fight, but instead on the fight's outcome as a part of the story being told, *then* everyone involved has got it right.'

APPENDIX

Recording the Fight – John Waller

Fight Notation

When a fight scene has begun to take shape, I sometimes find it desirable to make a written record of the choreography, a copy of which may be passed on to the director, cast members and other relevant production staff. Speaking personally, I like to work as fast as possible with the fighters, and my system seems to ensure that most of them pick up and retain the choreography without much difficulty. My fight notation is therefore intended to serve as a memory aid and may be quite briefly written. Sometimes, however, I will set everything down in much more detail – for example, when I work on a theatre production scheduled for a long run.

Though there have been many attempts by various individuals over the years to put forward a universal written system for fight notation, most fight directors still prefer their own specialized methods. Of course, the problem with any idiosyncratic system is that what can be easily read by one person may completely baffle another. For this reason I am still convinced after thirty years that the most reliable form of notation is to write out the entire sequence longhand in a manner similar to that used over the previous pages.

For a complete record I always describe every physical action in a sword fight according to the position of the fighter's sword and body: when attacking, the target and type of blow come first followed by the foot movement, while for the defences the foot movement comes first and afterwards the block or beat. However I try to keep the directions as far as possible free of historical or fencing terminology, which I believe can be unnecessarily confusing. Neither do I follow the increasing tendency in the fight directing world to describe attacks and defences in purely numerical terms, which I believe distances the performers from their roles as fighters by requiring them to memorize moves using an abstract system, instead of one which allows them to clarify when necessary the physical logic of how their bodies are working.

Over the following pages are three examples taken from my original fight notation for the *Monty Python and the Holy Grail* and *Hawk the Slayer* films, as well as for Ian McKellen's stage production of *Richard III*. Though what is written may not be exactly representative of the fights as these eventually appeared on stage or screen, still you can see how, across a period of nearly twenty years, my basic longhand system has hardly changed.

Monty Python and the Holy Grail (1974)

Monty Python and the Holy Grail was the second feature film made by the Python team. Their previous film, *And Now for Something Completely Different*, was a compilation of sketches from the original television series, but for *The Holy Grail*, directed by Terry Gilliam and Terry Jones together, they certainly did have something completely different in mind. The end result was an anarchic retelling of the Arthurian myth, but one which sometimes gave a remarkable visual impression of the early Middle Ages.

In one scene, Graeme Chapman, as King Arthur, comes upon the Black and Green Knights in a forest clearing, fighting a pass-of-arms with two-handed swords. The pass-of-arms was a variation on the tournament (or medieval sporting war-game), during which men-at-arms tested their fighting skills by offering to hold a place, such as a bridge or crossroads, against all comers. Far from being a comic fight, however, the choreography was purposefully realistic and brutal, intended to give an impression of two warriors locked in a life or death struggle for the right of way. John Cleese played the Black Knight, Terry Gilliam himself the Green Knight, and – apart from the final moment – neither was replaced by a double for any of the action.

TERRY	Cuts at J's left side
JOHN	Parries blade up, and pushing back, cuts at T's left side
TERRY	Parries blade up and pushes back
Break	
TERRY	Makes sweeping cut from right to left at J's stomach
JOHN	Jumps back from T's cut and cuts down to T's right shoulder
TERRY	Parries blade right and sloping. As J's blade hits ground T closes and hits J in right side with left knee.
JOHN	Staggers back
TERRY	Puts left hand on J's right shoulder and pommels (past J's right cheek)
JOHN	Staggers back
TERRY	Cuts down to J's head
JOHN	Parries hand on blade, pushes T's blade up and hits T in stomach from right
TERRY	Doubles up
JOHN	Hits T on head from left
TERRY	Falls to ground, lands on back
JOHN	Stabs at T (point enters ground by T's right shoulder)
TERRY	Rolls left and regaining feet cuts down at J's right shoulder
JOHN	Spins away from cut

Break
JOHN	Thrusts at T's stomach
TERRY	Envelopes left
JOHN	Hits backhanded at the side of T's head

Break
TERRY	Thrusts at stomach (Make sure to leave legs wide apart)
JOHN	Envelopes right and kicks T in crotch
TERRY	Drops to knees

Reviewing my original fight notes I was reminded that when the notation was written, the fight was intended to be longer than the one that eventually appeared in the film, including a sequence with the combatants using flails and axes. The final move was the same, however, with John hurling his two-hander through the air to transfix Terry (doubled by myself) through the sight in his helm!

Hawk the Slayer (1980)

Hawk the Slayer was a sword and sorcery adventure produced by Harry Robinson and directed by Terry Marcel. The pair were enthusiastic about the project and confident that they could rival with a lesser budget some of the more lavish Hollywood fantasy spectaculars being made at the time. There was plenty of swordfighting, archery and even a duel with throwing axes. Fortunately the character of Hawk was played by a very physical American actor called John Terry. John immediately impressed me with his positive attitude: Hawk was in fact his first role in a feature film, and I'm glad to say he has gone on to make many other films since. I also got to work with Jack Palance, one of my favourite actors, who played the villainous Voltan.

In the film, one of Hawk's helpers is Gort the giant, played by veteran British actor and comic Bernard Bresslaw. In the following fight, Gort is surrounded and set upon by a party of soldiers, who he quickly finishes off using his own special weapon, a huge war hammer. Note the diagram, showing the positions of the fighters relative to the camera at the beginning of the fight.

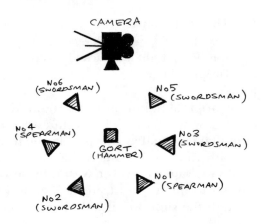

GORT faces camera
All SOLDIERS make aggressive but tentative actions

No. 1	Thrusts with spear at right side of Gort's back
GORT	Side-steps left with left leg, deflects spear with hammer (head down), jabs No. 1 in stomach with shaft end
No. 1	Staggers back
No. 2	Backhand cut at Gort's left
GORT	Steps back left leg and blocks with one hand on grip, one on shaft, kicks No. 2 off with left foot
No. 2	Moves left
No. 3	Cuts down at Gort's head, misses (behind back)
GORT	Spins to right on right leg, hits No. 3 in back with hammer with two-handed swing
No. 3	Falls forward
No. 4	Thrusts with spear at Gort's left side, misses
GORT	Steps back with left, grabs spear with left hand, pulls forward, hits No. 4 on back with hammer head
No. 5	Cuts down at Gort's head

GORT	Stands ground, blocks with left hand and hits in stomach with head of hammer
No. 6	Cuts at Gort's left side
GORT	Blocks with one hand on grip, one on shaft, hammer head down, and hits No. 6 in stomach with hammer head

Sir Ian McKellen's *Richard III* (1990)

I was impressed by the dedication Sir Ian McKellen put into learning this fight while wearing a replica fifteenth-century steel harness of the type men-at-arms actually fought in during the Wars of the Roses. Interestingly, the greater part of Richard Eyre's National Theatre production was given a dark, fascistic 1930s look, with Ian playing Richard as a sort of Oswald Mosley figure. An image from the period which proved inspirational was Hubert Lanzinger's painting *The Standard Bearer* which depicts Adolf Hitler riding in full armour. Because this painting was personally selected by the Nazi leader as his official portrait for the Great German Art Exhibition in 1938, the director decided to bring it to life for the final battle scene. I worked hard with Ian and Colin Hurley, who played Richmond, to achieve the desired result.

Both Ian and Richard Eyre agreed that the problem with so many actors who take on the part of Richard is that they feel compelled to play him with an obvious deformity, ignoring the fact that the play is set in 1480, when the essence of the knight was still to be a highly mobile mounted fighter. Just before the final fight, Richard cries, 'a horse, a horse, my kingdom for a horse,' yet a man with a withered arm and a gammy leg would be physically incapable of controlling a stallion in the heat of battle. Neither would he be able to fight in plate-armour. Even by the time the play was written in the last decade of the sixteenth century knights could still be seen riding in full armour, if only during tournaments, and Shakespeare cannot have intended Richard to

be played in a way that would prevent the audience acknowl-
edging what a great warrior he was. I believe that Richard's
deformity should be seen less in physical terms, and more
as a symbol of the character's failure to accord with the
medieval and Elizabethan image of the *parfait* knight, the
warrior who was physically and spiritually perfect.

RICHARD turns left upstage
FIRST FOUR of RICHMOND'S army run down stage-right
to face him
RICHARD turns with them
SECOND FOUR appear
RICHARD turns upstage, sees RICHMOND in the gap and
rushes at him
They fight
During the fight everyone should be aware that RICHARD
is like a wild boar surrounded by hounds waiting for the
hunter to finish him off
All keep tense – when RICHMOND is in danger close in to
help; when he recovers back off; change postures during
fight – adopt different aggressive stances

IAN	Cuts down at C's head
COLIN	Defends, sword point left, elbow right
IAN	Thrusts at C's groin (aim off upstage)
COLIN	Beats aside, blade down right
IAN	Backhand cuts left to right across C's stomach, then forehand cuts to stomach right to left
COLIN	Jumps back both times, then cuts down at I's head
IAN	Steps into the attack, blocks with sword, point left, elbow right, takes C's sword down right, barges C with left shoulder
COLIN	Staggers back stage-left
IAN	Cuts down at C
COLIN	Avoids by jumping back

RICHMOND'S soldiers move in

No. 1	Thrusts with spear at I's groin (upstage)
IAN	Beats, blade down left

No. 2 prepares to attack

| IAN | Swings anticlockwise and cuts right to left at No. 2 before he can attack |

RICHMOND is waiting, stalking, and seeing his opportunity, makes a two-handed cut downward at RICHARD's head (aiming off upstage)

IAN	Avoids by jumping downstage
COLIN	Cuts two-handed left to right at I's neck (aiming off diagonally over I's head)
IAN	Ducks and body charges C under his arms, knocking him up stage right, then thrusts at C's stomach (aiming off downstage)
COLIN	Beats blade down right and cuts at I's head
IAN	Avoids by stepping left foot behind right and pommels C on back of helm
COLIN	Staggers downstage

The final move of this fight was another memorable piece of brutality as Ian, hurled downstage on to his back by Colin, received a sword thrust deep into the genitals. This was a fate which must have befallen many men-at-arms and soldiers during medieval battles. The effect was simply achieved by Ian arching his back off the ground, allowing Colin's sword to slide underneath, but it was the reactions of both men, with Ian twisting his face to the audience as he screamed in agony, that really told the story.

There is of course one other important method of recording choreography that modern technology has provided us with: the video camera! If one of these can be obtained, a good fight rehearsal can be taped and subsequently viewed as many times as necessary to give the performers not only a mental but also a visual record of the choreography.

Organizations

The following organizations may be able to give further

advice and information on historical weapons training and/or stage combat. The names and addresses were correct at the time of writing.

The European Historical Combat Guild
Keith Ducklin
13 Jefferson Close
Ealing
London W13 9XJ
UK

The British Academy of Dramatic Combat
Andrew Fraser
9 Henley Drive
Rawdon
Leeds W. Yorks
LS19 6NX
UK

The British Academy of Stage and Screen Combat
Richard Ryan
10 Cranbrook Park
Wood Green
London N22 5NA
UK

The Society of American Fight Directors
Linda McCollum
Dept of Theatre Arts
University of Nevada
4505 S. Maryland Parkway
Las Vegas, NV 89154-5044
USA

Fight Directors Canada
Robert Seale (President)
39 Wheatsheaf Crescent
North York
Ontario M3N 1P7
Canada

Society of Australian Fight Directors
Nigel Poulton
91 Carranya Street
Camp Hill
Queensland 4152
Australia

The New Zealand Stage Combat Society
Tony Woolf
PO Box 38046, Wellington Mail Centre
Wellington
New Zealand

The following organizations can be approached for further advice and information on historical weapons training. The names and addresses were correct at the time of writing.

The European Historical Combat Guild
As above

The Historical Armed Combat Association
Website: *www.thehaca.com*
E-mail: webmaster@thehaca.com

Further Reading

For many years there has been a large number of books available on almost every aspect of sword development and manufacture. There has been virtually none written or printed on either the uses of the sword or its associated fighting styles. Thankfully, the resurgence of interest in Western martial arts means that copies of period fight manuals are now becoming far easier to obtain, especially via the Internet.

The student and enthusiast of historical swordsmanship or stage-combat can do no better than to acquire the following two excellent overviews of historical fighting styles:

Egerton Castle's *Schools and Masters of Fence*, George Bell and
    Sons, London, 1885
Arthur Wise's *The Art and History of Personal Combat*, Hugh
    Evelyn, London, 1971
Both the above titles are out of print but are sometimes
obtainable through book search companies. Be warned,
though: the cost can be quite high!
The following extensively illustrated manuals are among
those which might prove especially helpful to the reader
interested in further study.

Fifteenth Century

Hans Talhoffer's *Fechtbuch*, Germany, several editions
    between 1443 and 1467
Fiori dei Liberi's *Flos Duellatorum*, Italy c.1410

Sixteenth Century

Achille Marozzo's *Opera Nova*, Italy, 1550
Salvatore Fabris' *De la Schermo, overo scienza d'arme*, Italy, 1606

Seventeenth/Eighteenth Centuries

Andre Wernesson de Liancour's *La Maistre D'armes*, France,
    1686
Dominic Angelo's *École des Armes* (later reprinted in English
    as *The School of Arms*), England, 1763

At the time of writing, very few original manuals are available in modern English translations. However, extensive
commentary is regularly offered on different masters and
their works by individuals and groups such as the HACA
(see page 191).